EDITOR
Rebecca A. Martusewicz
Eastern Michigan University

MANAGING EDITOR
Maureen McCormack
Eastern Michigan University

EDITORIAL ASSISTANT
Michele Zehr
Eastern Michigan University

EDITORIAL ADVISORY BOARD

Sandra Spickard Prettyman (2005)
University of Akron

Mary Bushnell Greiner (2005)
Queens College, SUNY

Joe Bishop (2006)
Eastern Michigan University

Dan W. Butin (2006)
Gettysburg College

Jeff Edmundson (2006)
Portland State University

Wendy Kohli (2006)
Fairfield University

Richard Brosio (2007)
University of Wisconsin, Milwaukee

Sue Ellen Henry (2007)
Bucknell University

Eugene Provenzo (2007)
University of Miami

Denise Taliaferro Baszile (2008)
Miami University at Ohio

Gretchen Givens Generett (2008)
Robert Morris University

Bruce Romanish (2008)
Washington State University– Vancouver

E. Wayne Ross (2008)
University of British Columbia

Scott Waltz (2008)
California State University– Monterey Bay

Kathleen Bennett deMarrais (Ex Officio)
University of Georgia

PRODUCTION EDITOR
Laura Perratore
Lawrence Erlbaum Associates, Inc.

Eastern Michigan University

Taylor & Francis Group
New York   London

TABLE OF CONTENTS

ESSAY REVIEW

SUBSCRIBER INFORMATION

Subscriptions: *Educational Studies: A Journal of the American Educational Studies Association* is published six times a year by Lawrence Erlbaum Associates, Inc., 10 Industrial Avenue, Mahwah, NJ 07430–2262. Periodicals postage is paid at Mahwah, NJ, and additional mailing offices. Subscriptions for Volumes 39 and 40, 2006, are available only on a calendar-year basis. Subscription to the journal is included in the annual dues to the American Educational Studies Association (AESA). Correspondence concerning membership subscriptions or applications should be sent to Dr. Sue Ellen Henry, Department of Education, Bucknell University, Lewisburg, PA 17837.

Order subscriptions through the Journal Subscription Department, Lawrence Erlbaum Associates, Inc., 10 Industrial Avenue, Mahwah, NJ 07430–2262. Send information requests and address changes to the Journal Subscription Department, Lawrence Erlbaum Associates, Inc. 10 Industrial Avenue, Mahwah, NJ 07430–2262. Address changes should include a copy of the mailing label. Claims for missing issues cannot be honored beyond 4 months after the mailing date. Duplicate copies cannot be sent to replace issues not delivered due to failure to notify publisher of change of address. Postmaster: Send address changes to *Educational Studies,* 10 Industrial Avenue, Mahwah, NJ 07430–2262.

COPYRIGHT

Copyright © 2006, American Educational Studies Association. No part of this publication may be used, in any form or by any means, without permission of the publisher. ISSN 0013-1946 (print) ISSN 1532-6993 (online).

Send special requests for permission to the Permissions Department, Lawrence Erlbaum Associates, Inc., 10 Industrial Avenue, Mahwah, NJ 07430–2262.

First published by Lawrence Erlbaum Associates, Inc.

This edition published 2012 by Routledge
711 Third Avenue, New York, NY 10017
2 Park Square, Milton Park, Abingdon, Oxon OX14 4RN

This journal is abstracted or indexed in *PsycINFO/Psychological Abstracts; Book Review Digest; Education Index/Abstracts; EBSCOhost Products; Sociological Abstracts; Cabell's Directories; The Philosopher's Index; Family Index Database.*
Microform copies of this journal are available through ProQuest Information and Learning, P. O. Box 1346, Ann Arbor, MI 48106–1346. For more information, call 1-800-521-0600, extension 2888.

EDITOR'S CORNER

Greetings all! It is my pleasure to be bringing you this Special Issue of *Educational Studies* on the fifteenth anniversary of Jonathan Kozol's *Savage Inequalities.* Kozol's direct and assessable excavations of the way poverty is maintained and aided by an unjust system of educational funding and, more importantly, by the system of belief that justifies it over and over again have become cornerstones in social foundations classrooms for years. Every semester, I count on Kozol's searing descriptions to tip the scales of my students' outrage, to pull them up short and wake them out of their white suburban slumber. For all the criticism laid upon his work—too liberal, too emotional, too "journalistic"—there can be no doubt of its poignancy or its usefulness in getting the point across: This country is structured by, even dependent upon, fundamental inequality that leaves millions of families facing hunger; unemployment; poor housing; inadequate health care; and exposure to toxins in their homes, soil, water, and air. Inadequate schooling is, for Kozol, more than an added injustice. It is at the heart of the problem because it dooms the children of these families to the same life.

When Sue Books approached me with the idea for this Special Issue, I was more than enthusiastic. I have been reading Sue's scholarship on the impoverishment of young children for years, and I knew that this would be a great opportunity for *Educational Studies.* And I was so right! She and Amy McAninch have done a superb job putting together this issue. The articles use the groundwork laid by Kozol to push out the analysis of poverty and schooling, extending and deepening Kozol's work in ways that I am certain our readers will find useful. The book reviews give us fresh looks at some of Kozol's classic works, introduce his latest contribution, and also look at important related works. I am so grateful to both our guest editors, and to all the contributors for the attention to these issues, and for the terrific work they have done to bring this issue to us.

No need to comment further; you will all soon judge for yourselves and may indeed be choosing this issue for your courses! If that is the case it is available through Lawrence Erlbaum—just look for purchasing information inside the front cover. And now, it is time for me to turn my attention to the stack of student papers waiting here on my desk. Time to see what connections my students draw between poverty, racism, and ecological devastation ... another crop of prospective teachers to put our hope and faith in. My best to you all in your own work toward a better world.

Respectfully,
Rebecca Martusewicz
Editor

GUEST EDITORS' INTRODUCTION

Jonathan Kozol's *Savage Inequalities*: A Fifteen-Year Reconsideration

SUE BOOKS
State University of New York at New Paltz

AMY MCANINCH
Rockhurst University

This thematic issue of *Educational Studies* evolved out of a conversation at the 2004 American Educational Studies Association conference. At the time, we did not know that Jonathan Kozol's (2005) new volume, *Shame of the Nation: The Restoration of Apartheid Schooling in America,* would be forthcoming. However, we thought a fifteen-year anniversary reconsideration of the realities Kozol brought to public light in 1991 in *Savage Inequalities: Children in America's Schools* was warranted for a number of reasons. Both of us have repeatedly used *Savage Inequalities* in our social foundations courses, and we have found that it has few rivals in terms of its impact on students. Kozol's moral outrage coupled with his compelling prose make this book a particularly effective springboard for closer study of the structures of school inequality, racial segregation, and the beliefs that protect privilege.

Almost without fail, students inquire about progress since the publication of *Savage Inequalities,* expressing a faith that the conditions in East St. Louis, Illinois, or the South Bronx surely have improved. As Kozol (1975) points out in *The Night Is Dark and I Am Far From Home,* arguably his most biting volume, faith of this kind is a particularly effective form of self-deceit for the middle class. The contributions to this issue demonstrate that any progress toward social justice in America's schools has been erratic, at best. Arguably, the inequities have worsened, year after year.

Donyell L. Roseboro, Michael P. O'Malley, and John Hunt take us back to East St. Louis to revisit the school funding and political situation there since the publication of *Savage Inequalities.* Their fascinating examination of the contentious relationship between the local school board and a financial oversight panel appointed by the state illustrates a complex clash of values and interests, exacerbated by polarized media representations of the relationship. Lost in the decade-long struggle between the school board and the oversight panel over funding and control of District 189, they found, have been the voices of parents and their concerns about their children's educational well-being.

Maryann Dickar shares a history of Erasmus Hall, the famous Brooklyn high school, and its physical decline over the last few decades. Relying on "a critical pedagogy of place" as a theoretical perspective, Dickar examines the link between the social identity of the students attending Erasmus Hall and the condition of the school's physical plant. She notes, "The students arriving at Erasmus in the 70s and 80s faced very different circumstances, had different historical experiences and a different relationship to schooling than those who had come before them. Much of their struggles are left out of the narrative of decline that popularly describes the school's deterioration." Instead, in a narrative that "glorifies the past and derides the present," the newer students are blamed for the school's decline, and the socially induced damage to the surrounding community is thereby rendered invisible.

Jane Fowler Morse examines litigation in New York over equity in school funding. Her case study of the progress of *Campaign for Fiscal Equity v. State*, focused on the New York City schools, provides a detailed look at one state's efforts to translate the language of state constitutional provisions into funding formulas in a post-*Rodriquez* era. After offering a compelling account of the litigation and subsequent legislative foot-dragging, Morse surmises that "nothing much has happened yet" to provide students in the New York City schools with the equitable funding they deserve as a foundation of equal educational opportunity.

While Morse focuses on one state's school funding litigation, Deborah A. Vestegen, Kristan Venegas, and Robert Knoeppel offer a broader survey of school funding litigation across the country in recent years. In what has been termed the "new wave" of school litigation at the state level, courts have tended to focus on the *adequacy* of funding rather than its equity. Verstegen and her colleagues argue that, as a qualitative standard, adequacy provides some protection against an "equality of poverty" in which schools are funded equally but at a bare minimum. At the same time, their comprehensive analysis of state litigation leads them to conclude that "schools in America are rich, they are poor, they are unequal and inadequate."

Five book reviews are included in this issue. Amy Stuart Wells reviews Kozol's most recent book, *Shame of the Nation*, and highlights his argument that "changes neither in school funding nor in the popular high-stakes accountability policies will solve the problem of apartheid schooling and the inequality it perpetuates." In her review of two new books on funding and school reform, Peter Schrag's *Final Test* and Richard Rothstein's *Class and Schools*, Molly Townes O'Brien similarly notes that "the separation of children into neighborhood schools—poor schools in poor neighborhoods and wealthy schools in wealthy neighborhoods—perpetuates privilege for some and 'lower class' status for others."

In other reviews, Louis Crouch, a research vice president at the Research Triangle Institute who advised the South African government on postapartheid educational reform, reviews the democratic government's first major self-assessment of public school reforms. Concerted attempts in South Africa to reduce funding disparities arguably have been much more successful than our own half-hearted efforts in the United States. Finally, in two reconsiderations, Raquel Farmer-Hinton, who attended the East St. Louis schools, looks again at *Savage Inequalities* and takes us back to the "Does money matter?" debate of the Coleman Report (1966), and Sabrina Ross considers David Purpel and William McLaurin's *Reflections on the Moral and Spiritual Crisis in Education*—a reprint and reconsideration of Purpel's 1989 book, *The Moral and Spiritual Crisis in Education.*

We hope these articles and reviews invite continued thought about the "savage inequalities" that condemn generation after generation of poor children and children of color to second-class status in a nation that, unlike South Africa, seemingly is shamed neither by its "restoration of apartheid schooling" nor by persistent disparities in the material foundations of educational opportunity. We also hope that the moral outrage expressed throughout the volume compels a few more of us to see in the nation's "shame" the possibility of heading in a profoundly different direction.

Acknowledgments

We would like to thank many people for helping to make this special issue of *Educational Studies* possible: certainly all of the contributors but also all those who submitted fine manuscripts that we unfortunately were unable to publish. As always, difficult decisions were necessary. We thank Rebecca Martusewicz for her enthusiasm when we first suggested the idea for this special issue and for her support and guidance in bringing it to fruition, and Ann-Marie Carmody for her editorial assistance.

References

Coleman, James S. 1966. *Equality of Educational Opportunity.* Washington, D.C.: U.S. Department of Health, Education, and Welfare, Office of Education.
Kozol, Jonathan. 1975. *The Night Is Dark and I Am Far from Home.* New York: Houghton Mifflin.
Kozol, Jonathan. 1991. *Savage Inequalities: Children in America's Schools.* New York: HarperCollins.
Kozol, Jonathan. 2005. *The Shame of the Nation: The Restoration of Apartheid Schooling in America.* New York: Crown Books.

ARTICLES

Talking Cents: Public Discourse, State Oversight, and Democratic Education in East St. Louis

DONYELL L. ROSEBORO
Southern Illinois University Edwardsville

MICHAEL P. O'MALLEY
Southern Illinois University Edwardsville

JOHN HUNT
Southern Illinois University Edwardsville

Since Jonathan Kozol's 1991 publication of *Savage Inequalities: Children in America's Schools*, East St. Louis, Illinois, District 189 has endured unswerving criticism and study. While Kozol's work made publicly known the horrible conditions of schools in the district, it did not bring immediate relief. In 1994, the state appointed a financial oversight panel to review the work of the local school board and to begin work on the district's budgetary problems. For the next ten years, this panel controlled all fiscal decisions for the schools in East St. Louis. District 189 moved from having a $5 million deficit and a total operating budget of $72 million to having $20 million in reserve funding and a $92 million operating budget. Using newspaper articles, state oversight panel reports, and budgetary data, we explore the tenuous, and at times untenable, public relationship between the local school board and the financial oversight committee.

We are visitors, waiting. We wait for the children to come forth, for their performances to astound us, as they must. We know what they do not know, that the standing ovation is guaranteed, that the audience will applaud their achievement. We are educators bound by a silent expectation that we must, at least appear to, love children. It is this code, this unspoken rule that guides our interpretations, opens our eyes, admonishes our critique, and moves us to cheer. Here, in this multi-million dollar facility, we watch these children perform for a crowd that looks back with white eyes. What does it mean for these honey/chocolate/almond skinned young people to dance before us—an us that gazes with false promise? Do our cheers sound hollow and contrived or meaningful and sincere? In those brief moments, as they dance, they are present and we are engaged, connected in an unspoken political struggle which makes this dance much more than a dance. We wonder if anyone notices that they are dancing for their lives.

Public Identities in East St. Louis

As outsiders looking in, we watched the children in the performing arts programs of the East St. Louis Center bring us into their world and for these moments, it was a world replete with laughter, love, and hope. At the time, it seemed quite different from the impoverished East St. Louis we had come to expect. Here, within the walls of the East St. Louis Center, a center with ties to Southern Illinois University Edwardsville, these children seemed quite capable of creating possibilities. Although the performances on this day were all designed to highlight the success of the programs and their indisputable impact on the children of East St. Louis, for us, all three faculty members at Southern Illinois University Edwardsville, they came to represent much more. And when one young man queried afterward, "Are you coming to teach us?" we felt compelled to reconsider our notions of public education in East St. Louis and our hope of doing research in what has come to be termed "beleaguered" District 189.

When Jonathan Kozol (1991) began his story of racial apartheid in America's schools with the publication of *Savage Inequalities*, he started with East St. Louis, Illinois. Historically, the town, located next to Missouri and just across the Mississippi River, emerged as a hub for river trade, railroad activity, and settlers flowing west in the early 1900s.[1] Ever since Lewis and Clark set forth through the area in the early 1800s, it has celebrated being a "gateway to the west." But, as is typical, this celebration in American history ignores the takeover of Native American land and black flight to the midwest; neither of these seems to be the stuff of legend. By 1917, with thousands of rural black farmers from the South arriving in the area, East St. Louis had become a multiracial and ethnic city struggling to collectively define its Native American, French, English, Spanish, German, Czech, and African American heritage. The year 1917 would also bear witness to one of the most violent confrontations between blacks and whites when fighting ensued as angry whites attacked black strike-breakers.

In October of 1994, three years after the publication of Kozol's widely acclaimed work, District 189 schools faced a projected budgetary deficit of between $5 million and $9 million. State education officials voted to take over control of the district and established a three-member oversight panel. They selected Richard J. Mark as chair and Saundra J. Hudson, a member of the Edwardsville Illinois Board of Education, and Robert Oakes, former superintendent of Decatur schools, as members. Because the state superintendent appointed the oversight panel against the wishes of the local school board, tensions between the two began immediately.

Historically, East St. Louis School District 189 has been one of the largest employers in the community. Membership on the Board of Education had long been seen as achieving a significant level of prestige and influence in the community. Although school board[2] members enjoyed an elevated status in the community, this status generally carried an attendant expectation of *quid pro quo* from supporters and constituents. It was commonly believed that school board members should use their individual and collective influence not only to award contracts to local bidders but also to employ as many local candidates as possible to fill both certified and support positions in the district.

The state superintendent appointed the oversight panel, however, in response to perceived waste and inefficiencies in the construction and management of the budget by the school system. With an accounting focus, the panel entered the district holding the belief that the students of District 189 would be better served by a more efficient use of the funds available to the school district. Speaking the language of *accountability*, the panel expressed concern for money and management. They equated improvement in school finances with improvement in learning environments. In contrast, the school board emphasized *total community*. They believed that contracts and jobs should go to businesses in East St. Louis to create sustainable economic development. The panel did not understand the language of total community that the board spoke and, in fact, interpreted this language as nepotism and favoritism. The school board, with equal vehemence, rejected the oversight panel's accountability concerns as an unwarranted intrusion from a group who knew nothing about the community.

As we worked to research the period of financial oversight, this ideological difference surfaced as one that seemed best able to explain the public discord between District 189's school board and oversight panel members. But, as we delved more deeply, we discovered a particular hesitancy from the citizens of East St. Louis who survived, witnessed, and critiqued the years of fiscal oversight. They were wary of strangers purporting to "do research." They are tired of being, in their words, spectacled by the media. Kozol's name is rarely mentioned here by people other than other academics. It is as if he came, he reported, and he was erased. To then revisit his seminal work requires a rethinking of how we do and define research. It requires persistent attention to the interaction of conflicting ideologies— frameworks of meaning that are almost impossible to penetrate and between which there is little common language. It is thus our aim in this preliminary study to examine what became a public drama between the school board and state appointed oversight panel. It was a political performance that highlighted, ignored, and masked the children in East St. Louis.

In addition, the question of spectacle, the public performance of identity, has profound implications for our theoretical understanding of democratic public education and our ability to translate or uncover meaning in America's public schools and current educational discourse. Media representations, while they may not reflect people's everyday identities, do name, classify, and label people in ways that disseminate public meaning. In gazing upon the "other," we invariably refashion and remake. We see media representations as "those people" and forget that they are interpretations in the making. In our analysis of media representations of relations between the East St. Louis school board and the financial oversight panel, we are particularly interested in the identities that came forth through the media and the practical as well as theoretical implications of these interpreted performances.

Perhaps more importantly, as we keep with us the memory of the children dancing on that one particular day in East St. Louis, we remain cognizant of *representation*. Thus, our task in this article is not to belabor what is already known—the East St. Louis schools are in need of repair, classrooms are sometimes not staffed, special education services are not up to par, and children do not score well on state standardized tests. Instead, we evaluate the public discourse between the oversight panel and the local school board. Because the oversight panel stressed the language of accountability and the school board stressed the language of total community, they each spoke an ideology different from the other. Each found it difficult to translate the other's motives and expectations.

To explore this ideological difference, we assessed the connections between public representation, school financing, and democratic education. To do so, we examined 175 newspaper articles printed between the years 1994 and 2004. Our goal was to evaluate how print media reflected, reinforced, and emphasized the ideological differences between the school board and oversight panel. In addition, we compared newspaper data to school financing patterns to determine the effects of these patterns on learning environments in District 189. Finally, we used data gleaned from newspaper articles, legal decisions, oversight panel reports, and state fiscal reports to assess evidence of democratic processes in the educational communities of East St. Louis.

Our theory is that the battles between the oversight panel and the East St. Louis School Board, highlighted in the media as a public battle between good (oversight panel) and evil (school board), reflect instead the complexity of democratic process, its problematic translation into current school infrastructure, and persistent tension between accountability and total community interpretive frameworks. While we identify and analyze accountability and total community frameworks here, we wish to emphasize the dynamism and multiplicity created by the interaction between those who operated with seemingly different interpretive frameworks. We do not suggest that accountability and total community frameworks are always mutually exclusive, but we do argue that the school board's and oversight panel's polarized relationship seemed to divorce accountability from total community. Each group's public discourse emphasized one interpretive framework to the exclusion of the other. Ultimately, we recognize that, through the media, constituents of East St. Louis came to have very public identities. Although these identities may not reflect the complex interactions that occurred on a daily basis and may not represent what the people of East St. Louis consider to be who they were and are, public personas do frame our analysis of the relationship between the board and the panel.

With this in mind, we understand identity in a postmodern sense, as constituted in time, space, and relationship (Anzaldua 1987; Butler 1993, 2003; Carlson and Apple 1998; Foucault 1997; Fusco 1995; Miller 2005; Mohanty 2003). It represents the "mundane way in which social agents *constitute* social reality through language, gesture, and all manner of symbolic social sign" (Butler 2003, 392). Identity as performed in public space thus forces us to examine how what we do is perceived, co-opted, and re-presented. Of greater importance are the effects these performances had on children and schools. Did they reflect, create, and enhance possibilities for transformative education, democratic education that engages the souls of children, that embraces challenge, and that responds to injustice?

Media Discourse: Epic Battles Between the Oversight Panel and School Board

When the oversight panel began its work in 1994, interim superintendent Katie Wright said, "The state is very displeased with our finances. It's a mess and I'm committed to try to work through it" (Gillerman 1994a, 1). Faced with an impending deadline and the possibility of not being able to pay teacher salaries through the end of the year, Wright and school board members proposed cutting 165 teaching positions and 65 other employee positions in what the *Post Dispatch* termed a "desperate money-saving move." In the same vein, Terry Turley, president of the East St. Louis Teachers Federation Local 1220, spoke to the more important consequence of the cuts: Schools that were already short-staffed would be even more short-staffed. Journalist Margaret Gillerman (1994) reported, "The state has encouraged staff cuts in the past saying the district's payroll is bloated with patronage hiring. The district is one of the largest employers in East St. Louis" (Gillerman 1994b).

Although the financial oversight panel had final authority over all the district's financial matters, it was this issue of hiring that illustrates the competing ideological frameworks driving both organizations. Despite the persistence of staff shortages each year, state officials repeatedly classified district hiring as "patronage" while local officials demanded that local people and companies be contracted to work with the district. By July of 1995, school board member Della Murphey complained about the district borrowing money from a Wisconsin bank instead of a bank in East St. Louis. She said specifically, "Keeping the money in East St. Louis institutions, as in past years, would do a lot for this community. Why are we borrowing the money from up in Wisconsin?" (Gillerman 1995, 2B).

If we analyze Murphey's point from a *total community* framework, then we interpret her concern as a legitimate one. In her stand for patronizing East St. Louis businesses, she becomes a champion for the underserved and underrepresented small business sector. If, however, we question her motives from an *accountability* framework, then we do not understand and cannot justify any business transaction that does not automatically preference the lowest bid. This ideological contradiction came forth continuously and, in February 2000, erupted when local contractors picketed the school board. The contractors, described as "angry" by *Belleville News-Democrat* reporter Mike Fitzgerald (2000), questioned the district's hiring of contractors with no black workers. After demanding to meet with superintendent Nate Anderson, members of the Metro East Black Contractors Organization negotiated a deal to have at least 35 percent of district construction or repair projects go to local contractors (8).

Although the school board approved the resolution, the oversight panel continued its criticism and, using every public opportunity, questioned the integrity of District 189 board members. In a report to the state board in September 2001, the oversight panel declared

> The culture of the district has been slow to change; Board members are more concerned about hiring local political associates than improving the learning environment and test scores .... The political pressures of jobs and contracts are just too pervasive for board members to be concerned about the real business of the district—education. We do not see that changing. The local board members too often act for personal and political benefits. (Financial Oversight Panel 2001)

Facing continued criticism by the oversight panel, school board members responded without hesitation. School board vice president Joseph Lewis rejected the notion that board members reacted to political pressure and, regarding the oversight panel's comments, added, "I think that's just a figment of their imagination" (Sultan 2001, A1). Lewis went on to say, "I don't know why they think they are the savior of these kids. They don't even know them. They are my nieces, my nephews." For Lewis and other board members, awarding contracts to local businesses and hiring local people for district jobs was not the result of "political pressure." It was, rather, their obligation to the community, which they felt was being inappropriately manipulated by outsiders.

Disputes between the oversight panel and school board entered the legal realm as well. In one instance, the panel fired 32 disaccounting firm, and in another, dissolved the entire school board. In the first case, brought to court by the East St. Louis Federation of Teachers, Local 1220, the trial and appellate courts both declared that the oversight panel had overstepped its authority in removing district employees, "absent an indication that the union employees are incompetent, dishonest, not readily available or otherwise incapable of performing tasks necessary for the panel to carry out its purposes" (School Law 1999, 1).

In the second case, brought by the school board and superintendent Geraldine Jenkins, the Illinois Supreme Court ruled that the panel had violated the due process of local board members when it, in essence, fired the entire board. At issue was the renewal of Superintendent Jenkin's contract. The board voted to renew, the panel rejected the contract renewal, and the board ignored the panel's directive. Following this rejection of the panel's mandate, the panel dismissed the entire board. Although the court determined that the oversight panel did have the authority to remove school board members, the justices upheld the board members' right to due process under the law. Since the panel did not provide such process, the dissolution of the board was in violation of the board members' constitutional rights (Sampen 1997).

In both cases, the legal arguments of the oversight panel and school board illustrate differences in their ideological frameworks. While both speak of process, the panel selects the language of management and the school board uses the language of democracy. The former reflects an interpretive framework of *bottom line* and *supervisory mandate* while the latter represents an ideology of *enfranchisement* and *participation*. The actions of both groups correspond with their different understandings. The panel, for example, chose not to notify board members of their removal, but, instead, simply informed the regional superintendent's office and ordered the vacancies filled. School board president Lonzo Greenwood spoke out against the dismantling of the board and said it would "undermine community involvement in the district. It all goes back to the community's right to govern its own schools" (Franck 1999). It is this question of governance that both explains and complicates any analysis of the relationship between the school board and oversight panel. While on the surface it would seem that this was just a battle for control of the district, disagreements between the two represented far more.

It was, for the school board, a battle to retain the right to make decisions for *their* children. It was about power. While we *do not argue* that the actions of the school board always, and without question, represented the best interests of children or the community, we *do argue* that the board perceived the oversight panel as an instrument of disenfranchisement designed to refashion the district without the input of community members. School board members throughout the United States are typically elected because they reflect the mores and values of the communities they serve. East St. Louis is no exception in this regard. Being an economically depressed community, the issue of employment for residents became paramount. It was standard operating procedure for school board members to employ as many residents as possible and to award as many contracts as possible to local firms. To have done otherwise would have been contrary to the norms of the community. We do, however, recognize that legitimate questions can be raised about the state's democratic right to intervene on the local level on behalf of all children but also caution that such intervention is complicated and rarely equitable, particularly when state oversight is imposed and not requested by the local community.[3]

By stripping the board of its authority and eventually removing its members, the state oversight panel, in effect, said (1) local citizens were not able to elect local representatives of character and quality; (2) local citizens did not have the right or wherewithal to reelect other, more appropriate representatives; (3) school board members did not or could not do what was best for their community; (4) any expectation on the part of community members that the school board should hire from within was political pressure (rather than a valid expectation since it was the largest employer in the area); and (5) the state board, whose members rarely visited the community, knew best. With good reason, the state superintendent appointed the panel to improve the district's finances but the action, no matter how well intentioned, sent the message that the school board and citizens of East St. Louis were incompetent. Once spoken, this message pervaded the media and community. It sabotaged the work of board members, superintendents, and oversight panel members. It was a message that could not be undone.

In fact, it was a message reinforced by the editorial board of the *St. Louis Post-Dispatch,* which used instances of teacher wrongdoing to implicate the school board and publicize its "incompetence." When athletic director Art May was indicted for embezzling money from the district, the *Post-Dispatch* editorial board ("Chance" 1997) had this to say:

> The facts apparently caught up with Mr. May. He was suspended last year as athletic director. Yet, as late as June, the school board was considering a $36,000 severance package for Mr. May. The deal was only scotched after word of the criminal investigation leaked out. Superintendent Geraldine Jenkins tried to take some credit last week for having asked for an inquiry into the athletic department's account. That takes a lot of nerve. Ms. Jenkins has been asleep at the switch, along with most of the school board.[4] (1C)

Aside from also publicizing the fact that oversight panel chairman Mark called Superintendent Jenkins "inept," the *Post-Dispatch* argued that the oversight panel was the primary ray of hope for the children of District 189. With an impending school board election the next month, voters in the district would have a chance to exercise their right to vote, oust corrupt school board members, and elect more competent leadership.

Between the media, school board, and oversight panel, words worked as weapons designed to target and destroy. While the board clung to its *total community* strategy, the panel held fast to its *accountability* policy and never the twain did meet. However, with some assistance from the media, the mini-war raging between the two emerged into the public arena with dramatic flare. To its credit, the *St. Louis Post-Dispatch* published a commentary in the midst of the ten-year feud.

In it, writer Julia Huiskamp (1997) outlined a long list of blame that could be divided equally amongst various stakeholders in District 189. Of herself and the media she said, "Even the voyeurs cannot escape censure: the media and people such as myself who look at the shambles with horror and fascination and make our livings telling the story. We are all to blame for sentencing many of District 189's 12,000 students to a life of marginalization and poverty" (B7). In this instance, this particular writer held herself accountable. For one moment, the polarization between oversight panel, superintendent, school board, and media faded from view and we were reminded once again that the children, those who seem least able to exercise power in these circumstances, are the ones most devastated by the board and panel's inability to communicate.

The media, as voyeuristic narrator, thus acted as the medium through which outsiders came to know the people of East St. Louis, but it also acted as the bridge that both separated and connected the citizens of District 189 to each other. Through the media, we engaged with their publicly constructed identities, came to know the citizens of East St. Louis, and questioned the accuracy of these particular representations. Although the identities that came forth through the media may be, at best, incomplete representations, they were the identities that demonstrated to the rest of the world how the people of District 189 manifested, negotiated, manipulated, and navigated institutional power structures.

Fiscal Effects of State Oversight

More important, we realized that this public spectacle between the school board and oversight panel demands a revisiting of the relationship between school funding and democratic education. Does increasing school revenue raise the possibility of creating democratic classrooms? Or, as some argued to Kozol (1991), does "throwing money at the problem" not solve anything? In a capitalist society, can public schools with less funding somehow create democratic learning possibilities? And, if our answer is yes, does that give license to the notion that school funding does not necessarily need to be equitably distributed? We, like Sue Books (2005), believe that patterned disparities in school funding do persist in our nation's schools and, most importantly, these disparities significantly undermine our ability to create democratic classrooms, spaces in which students and teachers work collaboratively toward the betterment of humanity.

While the political drama played out in the media, the state oversight panel and school board each worked to resurrect the district's finances. When the state superintendent authorized the oversight panel to take control of the finances, District 189 was in dire straits. Facing a multimillion dollar budgetary shortfall in 1994 and the impending prospect of having to borrow money to complete the academic year, the school board agreed to work with the oversight panel. When beginning its work, the oversight panel held as its initial goal to save the district from "insolvency." In its 2002 report to the state superintendent, the panel said, "The panel believes that the children of District 189 can be given a better learning environment, better educational choices and a well run educational program with the funding that currently exists" (Financial Oversight Panel 2002, 3). They believed that district funds were being mismanaged; board members spent a disproportionate amount of revenue on employment and spent very little on building maintenance and supplies.

Public schools in Illinois, like those in many other states, are funded through a combination of local property taxes, state funding, and federal funding. Illinois uses a system often called a resource equalizer approach to school funding. The higher the amount of local dollars contributed toward funding schools through local property taxes, the lower the percentage of the school district's budget that comes from state funding. The converse is also true. Article 10, Section 1 of the 1970 Constitution of the State of Illinois asserts that, "The State has the primary responsibility for funding the system of public education." Over the years, the legislative interpretation of "primary responsibility" has meant at least 51 percent should be funded by the state. In actuality, the percent of state funding varies greatly, depending upon the local contribution. Individual school districts may receive significantly more than 51 percent of their funding from the state, or significantly less.

In addition to local contribution, the major factor driving the amount of a district's funding from the state is student attendance. The average daily attendance of a school district, multiplied by a per-pupil designated amount by the state, gives a district its general state aid entitlement. District 189 has faced two major financial challenges over the years. First, the property values in East St. Louis are very low. Even though the school district has one of the highest tax rates in St. Clair County, this rate generates a relatively low level of funding from local sources. The state has thus increased its funding, up to a point. For example, in September of 2001, the financial oversight panel reported to the Illinois State Board of Education that 89 percent of District 189's revenues were received from state and federal sources; only 11 percent of the district's funding came from local sources that year. This proportion of local funding was fairly typical during the years of state oversight (Financial Oversight Panel 2001). On the other hand, the school district's enrollment declined every year except one between 1994 and 2004. During the 1994 fiscal year, the district boasted an average daily attendance of approximately 12,161 students. By the 2004 fiscal year, this average daily attendance had declined to about 8,845 students (Illinois State Board of Education 2005).

On the surface, such a decline would seem catastrophic to the school district. However, over many of the years between 1994 and 2004, the State of Illinois was able to increase the per-pupil level of funding provided to school districts. Therefore, while the general instructional expenditures of District 189 were $47,787,202 in the 1994 fiscal year, instructional expenditures hovered at $46,131,591 in the 2004 fiscal year. It is important to note, however, that District 189 was educating approximately 3,315 fewer students in 2004 than in 1994. Because of this decline in student population, per-pupil expenditures actually increased over the ten-year period. The bottom line: Per-pupil expenditures moved from just over $3,855 in 1997 to just over $5,215 in 2004 (Illinois State Board of Education 2005).[5]

Since District 189 is located in an impoverished area, it has also been entitled to significant levels of federal funding over the years. Specifically, No Child Left Behind funds such as Title I, Title II, Title IV, and Title VI have been available to the district. As a consequence, the percentage of District 189's revenues coming from federal sources has been creeping upward over the past several years. In the 2001 fiscal year, slightly more than 13 percent of the district's revenues came from federal sources. By the 2004 fiscal year, that share had increased to over 15 percent of overall revenues. This amounted to just over $15 million.

Over the years of oversight control, the Board of Education of District 189 frequently accused the oversight panel of overstepping its charge. There was a clear belief that the panel periodically became too involved in the "educational" issues of the district, as opposed to the "fiscal" issues. The panel interpreted its fiscal responsibilities broadly—they claimed control over all budgetary matters related to district operations, including the hiring and firing of district personnel. In contrast, the local school board and union officials claimed that the panel did not have such broad authority. During the course of the oversight, the Board of Education sued the oversight panel for overstepping its authority. Although the board was criticized in the media for "wasting" money, board members viewed their actions as necessary for democratic process. They felt they were protecting the community from an oversight panel that wanted to strip the citizens of District 189 of the right to govern themselves.

Democratic Process and Education: What Must We Sacrifice "For the Sake of the Children?"

> Swirling colors, rhythmic movements, Latino beat … these children who are dancing for their lives celebrate for us cultural fusions that even still remain, for many, little more than an unheard, unseen, misunderstood thread in the history of our great America. What do we feel in the midst of this magnificent performance of cultural harmony? What do these children feel? They enact a performance of hope, proclaiming through their staged positionalities a possibility of cultural healing, sharing authentic talent, demonstrating learning and growth taking place at the East St. Louis Center. Does this fleeting moment of hope assuage our progressive sensibilities, assuring us that a difference is being made and lives are becoming better? It is difficult to fathom that when we leave these children and the committed staff of this bright center, returning to the wide open forested hills and fields of our campus, that most of these children will go home to places of literal poverty and dire economic need.

During the ten years of financial oversight, teachers periodically went on strike, the school board sued the oversight panel, parents sued the school board and district, the oversight panel attempted to dissolve the school board, and the Federal Bureau of Investigation (FBI) launched an investigation into the district (an investigation encouraged by the oversight panel, which claimed that the district was entirely corrupt). While the media and oversight panel charged the school board with fiscal waste and mismanagement, what happened to the children in the district? How were their lives altered by state oversight and what, if any, improvement occurred in education?

Four months earlier than expected, the state superintendent announced an agreement with the district school board in which he would dissolve the oversight panel. Panel Chairman Mark's public response was, "I was pretty shocked that they are going to do this without ever discussing any of the details with the financial oversight panel" (Aguilar 2004). In retrospect, the ten years of financial oversight were marked by lack of stability, sustainable leadership, and planned change. In 1997 Superintendent Geraldine Jenkins left her position among allegations that she was incompetent. Six years later the subsequent superintendent, Nate Anderson, resigned his position citing tensions with the school board and the oversight panel. This time, Mark told the *Post-Dispatch* he was uncertain whether the panel would have approved a new contract for Anderson and that "obviously, there is no administrative control in that district" (Aguilar 2004, B1). Despite structural and organizational reforms during the years of financial oversight, reforms that balanced the budget and brought in contracts for nine new and renovated buildings, the fiscal concerns were not entirely resolved through state oversight.

In East St. Louis, the appointment of a state oversight panel, while achieving a level of financial stability and capital improvements, did not generate an educational environment capable of facilitating significant academic improvement. Student learning and achievement remain significantly limited, as evidenced by student performance on state tests. For the 2003–2004 academic year, for example, only 31.7 percent of the students met or exceeded standards in contrast to the state average of 62.4 percent. In addition, while the state average posted a modest gain from the preceding year (1.4 percent), district achievement in reading, mathematics, and writing decreased at almost every grade level with an overall decline of 12.6 percent (East St. Louis School District 189 2004 Report Card, 3, 5–7). It does not appear that this academic disparity can be ascribed primarily to a funding differential in that the district and state per-pupil expenditures are comparable, with the state providing 74.3 percent of the district's 2002–2003 revenue.[6] What is clear is that a decade of state financial oversight and even state aid to create equitable revenue rates did not translate into significant improvements in academic achievement for the students of the East St. Louis school district.

As educators interested in democratic education, we enter the story of East St. Louis here to juxtapose it with the current debate among academic professionals who work with teacher- education programs. Although there is no universally accepted definition of democratic public education, many have argued that it emphasizes engaged learning, which takes place continuously in multiple contexts. Creating democratic learning environments demands that we pay attention to issues of justice and equity and that we conceptualize the school as intricately connected to the "real world" and not, somehow, a haven disassociated from it (Carlson and Apple 1998; Gutmann 1999; Hooks 2003). It is a concept of education in which democracy is about experience and process, one in which teaching and learning are forever linked; there is no latter without the former (Freire 1998).

For our purposes in this study, we question the relationship among media representation, school financing, and democratic education. Does media coverage, and, by implication, the identities it constructs, really matter? Does it effect notable change in the conditions of school children? Put more bluntly, media discourse established a clear "us" versus "them" framework in which the children of District 189 became both the objects and subjects of debate. Approximately two decades of educational research from critical theory, curriculum theory, feminist theory, qualitative inquiry, and queer perspectives have made it evident to the research community that dualities tend to enhance fragmentation and polarization (Kanpol 1998; Lincoln and Guba 1985; Miller 2005; Pinar et al. 1995). We see this research-based assertion borne out in the reform model used in East St. Louis. The model created a bifurcated governance structure that emphasized the hierarchical and adversarial nature of the relationship between the panel and school board.

In analyzing cultural and political situations of duality in which effective communication is impeded by empty rhetoric, Fusco (1995) observed that possibilities for border crossing become evident in "the voices of those marginalized by the official discourses of both sides" (19). While both the panel and school board claimed to have the "best interests" of children in mind, their public tensions made the students simultaneously invisible and hypervisible. The panel's inability to cross communicative borders and speak differently (in a language the school board could understand) and the school board's inability to do the same became a public representation that overshadowed the struggles of children in District 189.

When we searched for marginal or limited voices that transcended the official discourses of the school board and the oversight panel, we "found" the voices of parents. Generally not visible in the decade-long conflict between the board and the panel, and certainly not integrated into those exchanges as an integral constituency, parent groups emerged on several occasions to assert their own desires for their children's learning.[7] In two instances, parents expressed a serious lack of confidence in District 189's capacity to educate their children. In 1997, parents expressed their disillusion with the school board–oversight panel leadership when the St. Clair County Regional Board of School Trustees approved 6–0 a parent-organized request to detach thirty-six residences on the district's eastern edge and reassign them to two other districts. In reaching its decision, the regional board emphasized the significance of the district's lack of progress with test scores and recognized parents' fears about entrusting their children to the district (Maty 1997).

Then in 2000, when 72 percent of Fairmont City's registered voters (a Hispanic majority) signed a petition to detach from the East St. Louis School District (an African American majority) and join the neighboring Collinsville schools (a white majority). Fairmont City residents stated that their concerns involved the quality of education, safety of the educational environment, and efficient use of tax revenue (Fairmont City 2000). While a thorough analysis of variations of school choice is beyond the scope of this article, the depth of parent concern and initiative, revealed in their capacity to organize, is pertinent to our inquiry. The parents exercised political action as a way to interrupt the district's way of proceeding and, in doing so, made very public statements about their expectations of the school district and relevant state educative bodies.

In this way, parents of East St. Louis acted as public pedagogues (Brady and O'Malley 2004) teaching us, educational and political professionals, about *their* children (Delpit 1996). Implicit in their action is a critique of the school board, oversight panel, and other district officials. Parents hold them all accountable for the failure of the district to educate their children. Absent any clear indication of who could transform the district, parents acted as educational leaders. To understand the parents' actions, we must move beyond the cynicism that often attaches to critique (Kanpol 1998) and accept the social phenomena of parents' political interruption as an anomalous place of learning (Ellsworth 2005).

For Ellsworth (2005), anomalous places of learning are "peculiar, irregular, abnormal, or difficult to classify pedagogical phenomena" (5). While provocative and promising, they are difficult to see as pedagogy when we remain rooted in "dominant educational discourses and practices—a position that takes knowledge to be a thing already made and learning to be an experience already known" (5). It is the alternate perspective, the differing vantage point, that allows one to imagine pedagogy in new ways and thus to conceptualize parents as teachers and school board members, oversight panel members, politicians, and educational researchers as learners. In discussing the architectural and conceptual design of places of learning, Ellsworth (2005) highlights the significance of a pedagogical hinge that creates the experience of a learning self by "putting inner thoughts, feelings, memories, fears, desires, and ideas in relations to outside others, events, history, culture, and socially constructed ideas" (37).

We suggest that the potential of a pedagogical hinge exists in the anomalous place of parental dissent. Specifically, how might parents' hopes, fears, and demands for their children come into mutual relation with the outside political and educational structures, the social realities of the school system? A pedagogical hinge might appear if persons in positions of power choose to move beyond essentialized positions of self as authority and expert to, instead, a privileging of the *learning self.* We believe that this choice to embrace self and other as both leader and learner offers a possibility for shifting the dynamics of reified and adversarial discourses like those that marred the school board–oversight panel relationship. If politicians and educators identify and privilege the *learning self* above other professional identities, we will be significantly more capable of engaging the conflicts inherent within school reform and more able to move firmly, professionally, and passionately toward meeting the needs of students in multiple school contexts.

Finally, we emphasize the importance of public discourse to democratic processes and possibilities. In this particular case of state oversight, polarized media representations failed to capture the shifting dynamics of the relationship between the school board and the financial oversight panel. Instead, they constructed a simplistic portrayal of the competing ideological frameworks that shaped the debate. The period of financial oversight brought together very different constituencies, all of whom claimed interest in student needs, yet we cannot say that state oversight significantly improved conditions for children in District 189. At best, we remain hopeful that ideological shifts are possible, and we suggest that administrative personnel charged with school reform shift their interpretive lenses—moving from accounting, administrative, or authoritarian frameworks to *learning* ones. Perhaps in this way, we can find different spaces for transformative democratic pedagogy.

Notes

1. The town, originally home to the Cahokia Indians, was recognized as an official part of St. Clair County in 1818 and was given the name, Illinois Town (Moore n.d.). Also see Rube Yelvington (1990) for additional information on East St. Louis.
2. It is important to note that the school board changed membership during the ten-year period of state oversight. In one widely publicized election in November of 1997, voters in the district did not support three incumbents (Martha Young, Marlene Smoot, and James Ross). This information taken from Smith (1997).
3. The state of Illinois has placed seven school districts under financial oversight (including East St. Louis). In some cases (e.g., Cairo, Hazel Crest, Round Lake, and Venice districts), the local school board and/or district officials requested the intervention of the state. In other cases (including Livingston and East St. Louis), the state mandated the appointment of an oversight panel. Mt. Morris was the first district to have a financial oversight panel, but it was annexed to another district. Data compiled from Illinois State Board of Education Finance pages located at http://www.isbe.net/finance/default.htm, http://www.isbe.net/news/2002/dec17–02b.htm, and http://www.isbe.net/news/2003/jul3–03.htm, http://www.isbe.net/news/2003/feb6–03.htm, http://www.isbe.net/news/2002/oct17–02.htm, and http://www.isbe.net/news/2002/dec24–02.htm
4. Art May later pled guilty to charges of embezzling $90,000 from the East St. Louis High School Athletic fund and, in a separate case, pled guilty to fondling a 16-year-old female student. May agreed to cooperate in an FBI investigation of corruption in the district.
5. Information also comes from Debra Hemberger in an e-mail to John Hunt on September 8, 2005. Hemberger responded on behalf of the Illinois State Board of Education to our request for operating expenses per pupil, per capita tuition charges, nine-month average daily attendance, instructional expenditures, and instruction per pupil from 1994–2004.

6. 2002–2003 instructional expenditure per pupil: district, $4,960; state average, $5,022. Per-pupil operating expenditure in the same year: district, $8,860; state average, $8,482. Average state aid that year was 30 percent of revenue.

7. A lawsuit also was brought by parents and filed by the American Civil Liberties Union. In it, parents claimed that District 189 did not provide adequate, safe, or quality education and that the district should be dismantled. In 1995, Judge Richard A. Aguirre ruled against the parents saying that the court, in essence, could not legislate educational policy for the district (Goodrich 1995, 9A).

References

Aguilar, Aisha. 2004. "School Panel Will Be Ousted." *St. Louis Post-Dispatch,* 10 June. http://web.lexis-nexis.com/universe

Anzaldua, Gloria. 1987. "La Concienza de la Mestiza: Towards a New Consciousness." In *Feminisms: An Anthology of Literary Theory and Criticism,* edited by R. R. Warhol and D. P. Herndl, 765–775. New Brunswick, N.J.: Rutgers University Press.

Books, Sue. 2005. "Funding Accountability: States, Courts, and Public Responsibility." In *Critical Social Issues in American Education,* edited by H. S. Shapiro and D. E. Purpel, 25–44. Mahwah, N.J.: Lawrence Erlbaum Associates.

Brady, Jeanne F., and Michael P. O'Malley. "The Language of Ethics and Imagination in Educational Leadership." Paper presented at the annual Curriculum and Pedagogy Conference, Oxford, Ohio, October 27–30 2004.

Butler, Judith. 1993. *Bodies that Matter.* New York: Routledge.

———. 2003. "Performative Acts and Gender Constitution: An Essay in Phenomenology and Feminist Theory." In *The Feminism and Visual Culture Reader,* edited by A. Jones, 392–402. New York: Routledge.

Carlson, Dennis, and Michael Apple, eds. 1998. *Power/Knowledge/Pedagogy: The Meaning of Democratic Education in Unsettling Times.* Boulder, Colo.: Westview Press.

"Chance for East St. Louis Schools." 1997. *St. Louis Post-Dispatch,* 29 August, p. 1C.

Delpit, Lisa. 1996. *Other People's Children: Cultural Conflict in the Classroom.* New York: New Press.

Ellsworth, Elizabeth. 2005. *Places of Learning: Media, Architecture, Pedagogy.* New York: Taylor and Francis Books.

"Fairmont City Residents ask to Defect from East St. Louis to Collinsville Schools." 2000. *St. Louis Post-Dispatch,* 26 October. http://web.lexis- nexis.com/universe

Financial Oversight Panel for East St. Louis District 189. 2001. *Annual Report to the State Superintendent from the Financial Oversight Panel for East St. Louis District 189,* September. Illinois State Board of Education. http://www.isbe.net/finance/ESL/Annualreport01.pdf

———. 2002. *Annual Report to the State Superintendent from the Financial Oversight Panel for East St. Louis District 189,* September. Illinois State Board of Education.

Fitzgerald, Mike. 2000. "Protestors Demand More Jobs for East St. Louis, Ill., Minority Contractors." *Belleville News-Democrat,* 22 February. http://web.lexis- nexis.com/universe

Foucault, Michel. 1997. *Ethics, Subjectivity and Truth,* translated by R. Hurley and edited by P. Rabinow. New York: New York Press.

Franck, Matthew. 1999. "Superintendent Concurs with Report on E. St. Louis Schools," *St. Louis Post-Dispatch,* 7 December. http://web.lexis- nexis.com/universe

Freire, P. 1998. *Teachers as Cultural Workers: Letters to Those Who Dare Teach.* Boulder, Colo.: Westview Press.

Fusco, Coco. 1995. *English is Broken Here: Notes on Cultural Fusion in the Americas.* New York: New Press.

Gillerman, Margaret. 1994a. "Schools are Taken to Task over Finances; Illinois Board Bars East St. Louis District from Borrowing Money Until New Plan is Ready." *St. Louis Post Dispatch,* 21 February. http://web.lexis-nexis.com/universe
———. 1994b. "230 Employee Cuts Urged in East St. Louis Schools." *St. Louis Post-Dispatch,* 26 March. http://web.lexis-nexis.com/universe
———. 1995. "E. St. Louis Schools Move to Avert Money Emergency; Board OKs Borrowing Plan, Officials Accept Wage Freeze." *St. Louis Post-Dispatch,* 25 July. http://web.lexis-nexis.com/universe
Goodrich, Robert. 1995. "Judge Rejects ACLU'S Suit over Schools in E. St. Louis." *St. Louis Post-Dispatch,* 7 September. http://web.lexis- nexis.com/universe
Gutmann, Amy. 1999. *Democratic Education.* Princeton, N.J.: Princeton University Press.
Heron, John, and Peter Reason. 1997. "A participatory inquiry paradigm." *Qualitative Inquiry* 3:274–294.
hooks, bell. 2003. *Teaching Community: A Pedagogy of Hope.* New York: Routledge.
Huiskamp, Julia. 1997. "Plenty of Blame for East St. Louis Schools," *St. Louis Post-Dispatch,* 18 November. http://web.lexis-nexis.com/universe
Illinois State Board of Education. 2005. *Data Analysis and Report Card, 1994–2004,* September 17. http://www.isbe.net/research/htmls/report_card.htm
———. *East St. Louis School District 189 2003 Report Card.* ftp://ftpirptcard.isbe.net/ReportCard2003/500821890_e.pdf
———. *East St. Louis School District 189 2004 Report Card.* ftp://ftpirptcard.isbe.net/ReportCard2004/500821890_e.pdf
Illinois State Constitution. "Article X: Education." http://www.ilga.gov/commission/lrb/con10.htm
Kanpol, Barry. 1998. *Teachers Talking Back and Breaking Bread.* New York: Hampton Press.
Kozol, Jonathan. 1991. *Savage Inequalities: Children in America's Schools.* New York: HarperPerennial.
Lincoln, Yvonna S., and Egon G. Guba 1985. *Naturalistic Inquiry.* Beverly Hills, Calif.: Sage Publications.
Maty, Joseph G. 1997. "Residents Flee District 189; Neighborhood's Children Get OK to Attend Other Schools." *St. Louis Post-Dispatch,* 9 June. http://web.lexis-nexis.com/universe
Miller, Janet. L. 2005. *Sounds of Silence Breaking: Women, Autobiography, Curriculum.* New York: Peter Lang Publishing.
Mohanty, Chandra T. 2003. *Feminism Without Borders.* Durham, N.C.: Duke University Press.
Moore, Arthur W. n.d. "The Birth of East St. Louis." East St. Louis Action Research Project. http://www.eslarp.uiuc.edu/ibex/archive/guidebook/birth.htm
Pinar, William, William Reynolds, Patrick Slattery, and Peter Taubman.1995. *Understanding Curriculum: An Introduction to the Study of Historical and Contemporary Discourses.* New York: Peter Lang Publishing.
Sampen, Don R. 1997. "School Board's Ouster Improper, Court Says," *Chicago Daily Law Bulletin,* 20 November. http://web.lexis-nexis.com/universe
School Law—Non-Union Hiring Appellate Summary. 1999. *Chicago Daily Law Bulletin,* 11 February.
Smith, Bill. 1997. "Voters in Troubled District Toss Out Three Incumbents; Winners Pledge Back to Basics." *St. Louis Post-Dispatch,* 5 November. http://web.lexis-nexis.com/universe
"State Board Approves Oversight Panel for Cairo School District." 2003. *Illinois State Board of Education News,* 6 February. http://www.isbe.net/news/2003/feb06–03.htm
"State Board Approves Oversight Panel for Hazel Crest." 2002. *Illinois State Board of Education News,* 17 October. http://www.isbe.net/news/2002/oct17- 02.htm
"State Board of Education Considers Financial Oversight Panel for Livingston School District." 2002. *Illinois State Board of Education News,* 17 December. http://www.isbe.net/news/2002/dec17–02b,htm

"State Superintendent Appoints Three-Member Oversight Panel for Venice School District." 2003. *Illinois State Board of Education News,* 3 July. http://www.isbe.net/news/2003/jul3–03.htm

Sultan, Aisha. 2001. "Panel Opposes Giving Money Control to East St. Louis Board; School Board Members Act from Personal, Political Interest Report Says," *St. Louis Post-Dispatch,* 22 February. http://web.lexis-nexis.com/universe

Yelvington, Rube. 1990. *East St. Louis: The Way It Is.* Mascoutah, Ill.: Top's Books.

Correspondence should be addressed to Donyell Roseboro, Department of Educational Leadership Campus Box 1125, Southern Illinois University, Edwardsville, IL 62026. E-mail: drosebo@siue.edu

Reading Place: Learning from the Savage Inequalities at Erasmus Hall

MARYANN DICKAR
New York University

Through his detailed descriptions of schools across America, Kozol (1991) demonstrated the symbolic impact of the physical space of schools with disturbing examples of institutionalized racism made visible. Thus, *Savage Inequalities* also initiated a critical pedagogy of place by questioning the relationship of racial identity to the quality and condition of physical spaces in schools. This essay historicizes and deepens such an analysis through a critical exploration of space and place at Erasmus Hall High School in Brooklyn, New York, and notes how institutionalized racism is enacted in schools and how it informs student experience.

Fifteen years ago, Jonathan Kozol (1991) reminded the nation about the "savage inequalities" in America's schools. In vivid detail, he not only noted the disparities in funding between city schools and their suburban neighbors but also demonstrated what those disparities meant in the experiences of students. Through detailed descriptions of schools across America, Kozol revealed how these public spaces have become decisively raced and classed, calling attention to segregation and to the disturbing lack of resources in schools serving black and Latino students. Beyond the powerful case he made for redistributing school funds, his analysis included the symbolic impact of physical space through examples of institutionalized racism made visible. Thus, *Savage Inequalities* also initiated a critical pedagogy of place by questioning how the social identity of students related to the quality and condition of the physical spaces in which they are educated.

A critical pedagogy of place reveals the environmental embodiment of inequality. By doing so, it questions the often taken-for-granted aspects of our physical world. Gruenewald (2003) argues that such a pedagogy understands that place

> is an expression of culture and that it represents the outcome of human choices and decisions, that its present state is one of many possible outcomes. When we fail to consider places as products of human decisions, we accept their existence as noncontroversial or inevitable, like the falling of rain or the fact of the sunrise …. Thus, places produce and teach particular ways of thinking about and being in the world. They tell us the way things are, even when they operate pedagogically beneath a conscious level. (627)

In this regard, a critical pedagogy of place asks why places are as they are, why they mean what they mean to us, and how they came to be that way. Rather than accept the notion that urban schools are dilapidated and poorly resourced because that is the nature of urban schools, Kozol exposed the policies that created such places. According to him, funding systems, particularly the linking of school funds to property taxes, isolate poor and minority students from their white and more affluent peers and structure the racialization of space.

This essay historicizes and deepens the analysis begun by Kozol through a critical exploration of place at Erasmus Hall High School in Brooklyn, New York. This analysis suggests how institutionalized racism is enacted in schools and how it informs student experience. By calling attention to institutionalized racism, I examine how racism is perpetuated through social practices that do not appear to be racist on the surface but which operate to support white interests or to undermine those of black students. At Erasmus, narratives and practices that linked the decline of the school to its black student population while preserving a glorified notion of the white past masked political decisions, public policies, and school practices that diminished the prospects of black students.

The Setting

Erasmus Hall Academy, in the Flatbush section of Brooklyn, opened its doors in 1787, making it the oldest school in New York State and the second oldest in the nation. Its original Dutch Colonial schoolhouse still stands in the center of the school's courtyard today. In 1896, the academy was deeded to the city of Brooklyn and made into a public high school, free and open to all. (Girls were admitted in 1801.) That year (1896), 150 students attended. By 1901 the student population grew enormously to 2,000. This massive growth followed the rapid development of Brooklyn after the consolidation of New York City in 1898[1] and the simultaneous development of high school as a popular institution rather than an elite one (Tyack and Hansot 1990; Spring 2001). To accommodate this significant growth and as part of his plan to establish a premier high school in each borough, New York's school superintendent and chief architect, C. B. Snyder, designed the Erasmus campus to echo the great schools of Europe. In 1906, the first of four new wings, the one on Flatbush Avenue, was completed. By 1939, the Bedford Avenue wing fully enclosed the original Academy building within a quadrangle in the manner of the residential colleges of Oxford and Cambridge, including Tudor architecture and impressive arches. Today, lush green grass still carpets the quadrangle surrounding the old Dutch schoolhouse in a sanctuary of calm and contemplation. In 1966 this original academy building was designated a New York City landmark and in 1975 was entered into the National Register of Historic Places. Later, the original building was renovated and turned into a museum with no classes meeting in this hollowed space. In 2003, the four surrounding wings were also designated as New York City landmarks.

As the history of the buildings suggests, Erasmus was known not only for its striking beauty but also for its outstanding academic reputation. It produced a long roster of accomplished alums including Pulitzer Prize winner Bernard Malamud; Nobel Laureate Barbara McClintock; former New Jersey Governor Jim Florio; and singers Eddie Cantor, Neil Diamond, and Barbra Streisand. However, by the early 1970s the school's reputation changed. The city's fiscal crisis[2] made maintenance of the large physical plant a low priority. No substantive repairs were made to the aging buildings for almost 20 years until 1993. When renovation finally began, workers discovered that the towers facing Flatbush and Bedford Avenues were not structurally sound. The rest of the building was in similar decay. Paint peeled and cracked from walls and ceilings, windows were broken, desks were missing, roofs leaked, blackboards were cracked, and chairs were splintered. As the racial and ethnic composition of its students changed from Jewish and Italian to African American and Caribbean, the physical plant fell into terrible disrepair. In the midst of all these changes, Erasmus' outstanding reputation declined as well. By the early 1980s, Erasmus Hall had one of the worst academic profiles in Brooklyn and was reputed to be a large and out-of-control urban school.

The story of Erasmus Hall echoes the histories of schools examined by Kozol in this period. Notably, Morris High School in the Bronx, featured in the chapter in *Savage Inequalities* on New York City, also designed by C. B. Snyder, fell into similar physical and academic decline. In 1991, Kozol noted the connection between black and Latino children and the crumbling buildings provided for them by the City of New York. Erasmus suggests that these links are not coincidental but that, as urban schools served more students of color, public investment in their education and in cities in general declined.

By the time *Savage Inequalities* was published in 1991, Erasmus' drop-out rate neared 50 percent and its standardized test scores ranked among the lowest in Brooklyn (Lyles, 1992). By this time too, Erasmus was a segregated school with no white students attending. In 1994, after years of such poor academic performance,

Erasmus Hall was restructured. The school, which served over 3,000 students (and as many as 6,000 in the past), was shut down and three new smaller schools were created. I taught at Erasmus Hall from 1989 to 1991 and then at one of the new smaller schools, Erasmus Hall Campus High School for Humanities, from 1996 to 2000.

The Meaning of Place

As Kozol documented in interviews with students, broken and dysfunctional schools emotionally harm the children that attend them. Alternately, schools with good reputations and impressive physical plants inspire children while also conveying notions of their entitlement. These effects of space on children can be seen in Erasmus' history. For example, one student from the old Erasmus Hall, Jean Solow Adell, class of 1937, described her feeling about the building, remembered fondly 50 years later:

> I felt privileged attending Erasmus. The buildings themselves with their Gothic architecture, arches, the lawns and pathways, the statue of Erasmus, and the Old Building, made me feel as though I was attending a college of lasting renown.

In 1997, another student, Lisette (pseudonym), sat in my classroom and looked at the courtyard full of construction trailers still undergoing renovations. Deep in thought, she eventually said to me

> "I heard this school used to be mad nice."
> "It was," I said. "We used to have graduation in front of the white building (the common term for the original Academy building). There were trees everywhere. It was really pretty. Maybe the renovations will be done in time for your graduation."
> (Pause) "I doubt it. They ruin everything for us."

The renovations, well behind schedule and over budget, were not finished in time for her graduation in 1999.

These two vignettes suggest how students at different points in Erasmus Hall's history have interpreted the meaning of the campus. For Lisette, a black student attending a segregated high school in the late 1990s, the campus stung of institutional indifference, which magnified her marginality. For Jean Solow Adell, a Jewish graduate in the 1930s, the campus environment sent a physical message of inspiration that made her feel part of a great scholarly tradition.

Stories like these clarify that the places where schooling occurs convey deep messages about who students are and what they can be. For Jean Adell, the physical structure made her feel as though she were part of an academic community of "lasting renown." Erasmus for her was not merely a good school but one that linked her to thinkers throughout time. Lisette's reading of the campus suggests that she felt cut off from that scholarly tradition. Her melancholy response to the campus is informed by her awareness that the school "used to be mad nice." The physical decay still visible in 1997, the extensive scaffolding blocking the architecture from her view, and the fast and cheap quality of the renovations in the building visually undermined the lofty ideals encoded in the architecture. Her reference to the unnamable "they" who "ruin everything for us" suggests that she perceived that her experience of Erasmus was socially constructed, not merely an accident of circumstance. Further, her reference to "us" and not to "me" suggests that she saw her experience as part of a collective experience shared by her peers and most probably informed by their shared blackness. Like Lisette and Jean Adell, students read their educational environments and take away profound messages about who they are and what they can be in the world. By historicizing the meaning of place at Erasmus Hall, we can gain a greater understanding of the issues that face urban schools today as well as a deeper understanding of how savage inequalities undermine urban school children.

Sources

In order to understand the meanings Erasmus carries, I draw most extensively on a group of histories produced to celebrate landmark anniversaries of the school, particularly, the bicentennial third volume of *The Chronicles of Erasmus Hall, 1937–1987.* Unlike previous versions of *The Chronicles,* which generally focused on the history of the institution itself, the edition published to celebrate the school's 200th anniversary included extensive qualitative data collected from questionnaires sent to many alumni about their experiences at Erasmus and what it meant to them. Filled with numerous statements by alumni, excerpts from school publications, and many photographs, this edition offers a rich text to understand dominant narratives on Erasmus. Importantly, this edition also tells the story of Erasmus from its golden age to its more recent struggles and had to explain the school's decline. Although offering only one perspective on Erasmus, it is the most widely circulated one and is documented in great detail. In addition to *The Chronicles,* I also draw on newspaper articles and on my observations and research as a teacher at the school from 1989–1991 and from 1996–2000 after it was restructured.

Framing the Erasmus Tradition

Perhaps because of its once impressive campus or its wretched decline, the sense of place at Erasmus is powerful and inescapable. As in earlier editions of *The Chronicles,* the campus is used to frame the interpretation of the lived experience of the school in the 1987 volume. The first page opens with "The Memory," establishing the link between the physical place and its educational mission:

> The campus touched everyone who passed through it, striking chords deep in
> each heart. How does a place, a mass of stone and swath of green, come to mean
> so much? Perhaps the rich heritage of architecture and garden are the outward
> symbols of the inner longing for achievement. Perhaps it calls forth the venera-
> tion of the past that enhances the present and makes it meaningful. Perhaps it is
> the evidence, here in stone on stone, of the continuity of human knowledge and
> its extension across time. Surely, for each one in each generation, it has been the
> heritage and the covenant of Erasmus made visible .... Each Erasmian remem-
> bers that first view of the campus, coming in from Flatbush Avenue, through the
> shadowed, echo-y arch, to be confronted by the quadrangle with Desiderius
> (Erasmus) himself presiding. (3)

This introduction to the meaning of the place suggests the ways the campus itself defines the experience, education and tradition of the school. The Tudor architecture surrounding the Dutch Colonial building articulates the heritage—makes the "covenant visible"—and romantically connects the students who have gone there with "the continuity of human knowledge," which is implicitly the knowledge of Europe. Through the power of the place itself, generation after generation of students can fulfill the "inner longing" for knowledge and enhancement—their inheritance of the Western tradition.

Rhetorically this passage suggests that this tradition is available to anyone who passes through the "shadowed, echo-y arch" and therefore is universal; however, the tradition is historically and culturally specific. In the early twentieth century, "Americanization" (inculcating European immigrants with American culture, behaviors and values) was a central objective of the New York City school system. The American culture immigrants were schooled in was unabashedly white, Anglo-Saxon, and Protestant (Tyack 1974; Spring 2001). The decision to design Erasmus Hall with such a strong visual connection to Anglo-Saxon culture was no doubt part of this effort. For the predominantly Jewish students who attended in the school's hey-day, the school may have provided access to the cultural capital of a white American identity to which they did not otherwise have access (Brumberg 1986). However, when students were visibly not European, their relationship to the Erasmus tradition became much more problematic as enacted through decisions about the use of the campus.

Although "The Memory" draws heavily on the transformative power of the visual campus, access to that sublime experience has been largely denied to the black students attending since the 1970s. In the early 1970s, wrought-iron gates were installed to prevent entry from the street because of safety concerns. Students were no longer allowed to enter through the fabled arches and instead were funneled directly into the building through side doors, dramatically changing student relation to the school space.

More dramatic changes came in 1991 when Erasmus began "scanning," meaning that students had to be scanned for weapons before entering the building. Today, students enter through the cafeteria, which is in the basement at the back of the building (Bedford Avenue) where they go through full-body scanning by metal detectors. The main entrance to school now includes the hostile gaze of security personnel.

Further, as part of the renovations during the 1990s, a brick wall was built separating the grass lawn from the walkway at the Bedford Avenue arch. The four large dumpsters where the school throws away its trash line this new brick wall and block the view of the campus. The long-lost entry ritual celebrated in *The Chronicles* differs profoundly from the entry ritual students submit to today.

Narratives of Decline

Still, the Old Erasmus clings to the new Erasmus. Because of its long history, its location, and its 250,000 alumni (Lyles, 1992), Erasmus holds a lasting place in local lore—so much so that Lisette in the late 1990s was familiar with what the school used to be like. Her peers frequently repeated stories they had heard about the school's past, which was always markedly different than how it was at the time.

I was first introduced to the narrative of decline that surrounded Erasmus during my job interview there in 1989. The principal warned that one of the things that angered him most was to hear people tell students, "Erasmus! That *used* to be such a good school!" I was also consistently greeted by similar remarks when I told people where I taught and heard similar complaints from some of my colleagues. A teacher preparing to retire took me into her confidence and lamented, "I don't know, but I just don't think these kids are as smart as we were." By "we" she meant the largely Jewish students of the past. (She was an alumna.) Her comment remained with me because of its blatantly racist assumptions about intelligence but also because it was said not in frustration but in deep contemplation. It was the only way she could explain the significant changes that had taken place at the school. Her remark blamed the decline of the school's academic reputation squarely on the current students who she constructed as intellectually inferior. Such narratives implicitly racialized the school's history, coding the past as white and the present as black. Current students were well versed in these narratives and got the message: Erasmus was good when Erasmus was white.

These narratives are circulated not only by Brooklynites and frustrated teachers, however. They are widely circulated in newspaper coverage on the school as well. The front page of *The Daily News* of February 16, 1992 presented disturbing pictures of Erasmus Hall High School with the headline, "Halls of Shame: Erasmus Hall High, once a jewel of the city's public schooling system, is falling apart."

The story inside was entitled "Rotting Erasmus" and in large print declared, "Erasmus Hall High School, once a proud symbol of the city's public education system, is a sad shell of its former glory" (5). The text of the story itself began

> Erasmus Hall High School in Brooklyn is a chilling picture of decay.
> Mice scurry in classrooms where Barbra Streisand studied music—making nests in abandoned book closets. Students navigate through a minefield of rusted gym lockers where Hall of Fame basketball player Billy Cunningham prepared for big games (5).

The article went on to demand the long overdue renovation of Erasmus Hall. In addition to the need for a better facility, the *News* also called attention to the symbolic quality of the school building itself:

> Modernization of the school has been promised since 1988, when the late Schools Chancellor Richard Green was inaugurated at the 200-year-old institution and vowed to make it a symbol of the school system's revitalization.
> Instead, Erasmus Hall—like dozens of crumbling city school buildings—is a sad shell of its former glory. Its original wooden structure, now a museum with a statue of the Dutch Scholar, Desiderius Erasmus, still stands in the courtyard—a reminder of the school's grand reputation. (5)

A year later, *The New York Times* (Dillon, 1993) reported a similar story, in slightly less sensational fashion. *The Times* also posited Erasmus as a school of significant symbolic import:

> Erasmus Hall's current troubles are a blemish on an illustrious history … . The school has always been one of the city's proudest; illustrious alumni include Barbra Streisand, the chess champion Bobby Fischer, and hundreds of physicians and jurists. But like many schools, Erasmus Hall decayed rapidly after the fiscal crisis in the 1970s, which decimated the Board of Education's maintenance work force. By the 1980's, the school was badly dilapidated … . Its 200th anniversary, however, ignited a restoration campaign. "The 200th Birthday of Erasmus Hall is a celebration of all that is best in American public education, and of what it can yet become," former board president Robert F. Wagner Jr. wrote in a 1987 letter to *The New York Times*. (B37, 44)

These depictions articulate a central theme that shapes the work of *The Chronicles* as well.

Both newspapers explain the decline of the school through the physical decline of the campus. The past is consistently represented by references to famous alumni and the school's great academic reputation. The present is represented through the physical decline of the plant, which stands in symbolically for the high rates of school failure that are also part of that decline. The narrative in these press pieces suggests that the issues that shaped the downfall of Erasmus are cosmetic rather than systemic. They suggest that the restoration of the physical plant will hearken a restoration of all the other aspects that were great.

The narrative of decline focuses on the connections between the physical plant and the school's academic reputation but glosses over deeper problems. It masks a deeper disinvestment in public schooling as well as political decisions. For example, the narrative fails to note that some schools were maintained in this period. As Kozol noted in his examination of District 10 in the Bronx, where predominately white schools were well maintained, decisions about school funding and the distribution of scarce resources favor schools with white populations.

Defining Communities

The racially coded narrative of decline also excludes more recent students from the Erasmus tradition, suggesting that blacks are not part of it. The campus is constructed as a central aspect of the Erasmus experience, but student access to that campus has changed over the years. Prior to 1989, the building in the center of the campus housed the Academy of the Arts and was used for dance studios. Because the college and guidance offices were also there, students would move in and out of the building and onto the campus all day. However, like the rest of the school, the 200-year-old wood-frame building fell into terrible disrepair. Moved by this shameful situation, a group of alumni and teachers mobilized to have the original building restored. As part of the celebration of the school's bicentennial, philanthropist Mary Astor donated the funds for its renovation so that a museum of education could be opened in this national landmark. All student functions were moved to the un-renovated and crumbling main building. Students were no longer permitted in the academy building. Because they now had no business there, they had no reason to enter the hallowed courtyard itself and thus were virtually cut off from the campus and the historical building as well as the environmental messages of hope and ambition it had conveyed to earlier students.

This dramatic change in the way students could use the campus encoded the narrative of decline on the spaces of the school. At the time the academy was restored, it was the only part of the school that was *not* falling apart and the only space students were not allowed to use. Consigning them to decaying space heightened the link between students and decline. Perhaps it is fitting that a museum opened in the old academy because of the public obsession with the glamorous past at Erasmus. But tellingly, the museum did not include the experiences of the students attending at the time. Instead, the museum enshrined Erasmus' white past with exhibits on what going to school at Erasmus was like in the nineteenth century and a history of the school's founding by the elites of Brooklyn and New York, including Alexander Hamilton and Aaron Burr. It also includes a Hall of Fame that celebrates the famous alums of the past. Strikingly, many current students do not even know there is a museum in "the white building," as they ironically call it, because they are not invited in.

Black students were relegated to the broken parts of the school while the refurbished building in the center celebrated a past from which they were completely excluded. The sanctification of the original building marginalized students spatially at the same time that it marginalized them ideologically and historically. The spatial configuration served as a metaphor for the relegation of black students to the margins of the academic community, of academic subjects, and, hence, of American culture. The official work of the school taking place in the classrooms mirrored the unofficial curriculum mapped by the utilization of space, as many teachers at the time were opposed to multiculturalism and student-centered pedagogies. The campus that profoundly inspired earlier generations served to denigrate the students attending in the 1990s.

Although it is unlikely that the marginalization and denigration of students was the intended outcome of creating the museum, it embodied the white narrative of black urban decline. The perpetuation of this narrative undermines the educational aspirations of students attending today, as it devalues their culture, history, and presence. Even if no one in authority consciously acted to bring about Erasmus' decline, the narrative itself implies that the changed student population is at least partly to blame.

Decline and Community in *The Chronicles*

One of the greatest challenges facing the authors of *The Chronicles* was to resolve the contradictions between the celebratory image of Erasmus it sought to promote and the reality of the school in the late 1980s. They did not avoid addressing these years but did find ways to maintain what they constructed as "the Erasmus tradition" throughout these trials. Particularly, *The Chronicles* asserted a unified narrative rooted in the timelessness and the resiliency of the school's tradition. However, this narrative becomes hard to sustain as the authors try to explain why things went wrong.

According to *The Chronicles,* the 1960s and 1970s were the pivotal decades of tumult and change described in the chapter entitled "The Years of Challenge," which traces the events during the tenure of Principal Saul Israel. The "challenge" was specifically the challenge to the Erasmus tradition. This chapter is broken into four such "challenges": "Vietnam Protests," "Teacher Strikes," "Student Activism," and "Urban Problems." Between 1968 and 1972 student protests against the Vietnam War and against racism at home were fairly frequent. Two demonstrations were so turbulent that they forced the school to shut down. At other times, students stayed away in protest of the war or in solidarity with those who were attending citywide demonstrations. In 1967, Robert F. Kennedy himself spoke at Erasmus' graduation criticizing President Johnson's war policy against which he would soon launch his own bid for the White House in 1968.

In those same years, New York City teachers participated in historic strikes with significant racial overtones. In 1968, teachers struck to oppose the firing of predominantly white union members by decentralized school boards in the Ocean Hill-Brownsville district, who wanted to bring in more teachers of color. In response, the teachers union successfully shut down the schools for much of the fall semester of 1968. This intense conflict, a racial watershed in New York City history, made the years of Israel's principalship tumultuous. They included challenges to the eurocentric tradition called into question by the Civil Rights Movement and by Black Nationalist critics throughout the nation and at Erasmus.[3]

The section on "Urban Problems," however, specifically calls attention to the greatest challenge to the "tradition"—the shift in Erasmus' student population from white to black. *The Chronicles* opened this section with these words:

> Because of its location, Erasmus Hall was inextricably involved in the problems of the Flatbush neighborhood. Middle-class black families had been living in Flatbush for years, but now the neighborhood was becoming home to an increasing number of poorer black families. Besides this socioeconomic change, the late 60's was a time of serious problems in maintaining racial balance in the city schools. The Erasmus district was rezoned to include children from distant neighborhoods. Along with motivated, capable students came others, who defied the rules of Erasmus Hall education. They disrupted classes, wandered the halls, scrawled graffiti on the walls and even menaced other students. (245)

This explanation of "urban problems" employs a number of discursive strategies to separate the new students from the school's tradition. The authors suggest that the poor black students who began arriving in the late 1960s are not like *us*, are not from *our* community, and do not share *our* vision. Offering no further explanation of why poor blacks, as opposed to poor whites or middle-class blacks, were somehow more of a problem, *The Chronicles* relies upon racist constructions of black urban youth to explain the school's fall and to suggest that it declined because the quality of students declined.

In an earlier time, during the Depression of the 1930s, *The Chronicles* pointed out that the school's population was not only ethnically diverse but also economically diverse because students were drawn from poor, working class, and middle-class homes. In the 1930s, "Most knew it didn't matter nearly as much where they came from as where they were going" (62). School unity came not from ethnic and class solidarity but from shared goals. Although it didn't matter where poor whites came from, apparently it did matter where poor blacks came from. Not only did it matter where they came from culturally and psychically, the neighborhoods they lived in also mattered.

The text redefines the school community by suggesting that the rezoning to "maintain racial balance" in the schools brought geographical outsiders. These outsiders (although all of Brooklyn was once zoned for Erasmus) who did not live in Flatbush did not share the vision and seemed to "defy the rules of Erasmus education." By separating these "others," the newcomers, from the students who share the vision of success through education, who live in the right neighborhood and are of the right class background, *The Chronicles* links the tradition of academic excellence to only one segment of the present student population. The "motivated and capable" carry on the tradition, much hampered by the majority of the student body, who are unmotivated and not capable.

Importantly, this construction of the shift in student population suggests that the new students were simply bad students. They were not constructed as socially situated people whose academic performance was shaped by a wide range of socioeconomic, political, and cultural factors. The school got bad when bad students came to the school, and those students were poor and black. Thus, black students were defined out of the Erasmus community physically as well as rhetorically.

While the narrative of the school's decline in *The Chronicles* constructs the students as the primary problem, at another point it suggests that the institution bore some responsibility too. In an attempt to synthesize the social upheavals of the period—the teacher strikes, the fiscal crisis of the 1970s, and the demographic shifts that drastically changed Erasmus—*The Chronicles* noted:

> Taken together, the outside pressures on Erasmus Hall during 1964–1972 gravely wounded it. By 1972, along with other American institutions, Erasmus Hall had been seriously battered by the winds of change. Because Erasmus Hall sat in the midst of a changing borough in one of the world's largest cities, the forces of this turbulent era affected it perhaps more than other institutions. With its new black and immigrant students and its traditional stance on education, Erasmus Hall encapsulated the tensions of the entire New York City public school system. (245–246)

Earlier the authors had suggested that new students outside the Erasmus community brought about decline. Here they suggest that the school itself was not responsive to those students. The image evoked in this passage is of a school that stood still while everything around it changed.

At this time, students were demanding ethnic studies, black history, and Puerto Rican culture courses, so one way of understanding Erasmus' "traditional" stance is that the school's curriculum was eurocentric. This tension remained when I began teaching there in 1989. Not only did the new students not live within the same community they also did not identify with the European culture that is celebrated in the architecture, in school rituals, and in the curriculum. Thus, the institution so visibly linked to the scholarly traditions of the Western world was unable, or at least slow, to accommodate students who so visibly were not European. Their very presence presented dilemmas for educators whose response was generally to stand firm on traditions rather than change to accommodate new students in new circumstances.

Economic Change in Brooklyn

The authors of *The Chronicles* grappled with defining an enduring and unified community and tradition in the face of significant changes that brought students who not only were racially different but also did not accommodate to the institution in the way earlier generations had. To deal with the contradictions, *The Chronicles* "others" large segments of the school's current population. Although the authors note that "Erasmus Hall sat in the midst of a changing borough," these changes are not critically analyzed.

In the 1950s Brooklyn was a thriving industrial city with an expanding economy. It was also a multicultural city with segregated ethnic and racial enclaves who are often romanticized as hard working, full of heart, and devoted Dodger fans. Prophetically, although no team in the 1950s was more financially successful and perhaps no team ever will have the deep unyielding love of so many, the Dodgers left Brooklyn for suburban Los Angeles with bigger parking lots and a new stadium. The Dodgers leaving was symbolic of the abandonment of Brooklyn occurring at the time. Many white working and middle-class families soon followed, leaving black families to their fate in increasingly segregated neighborhoods. As whites and the Dodgers evacuated the vast residential terrain of Flatbush, new black immigrants from the Caribbean took their place in large numbers (Waters 1999).

The emerging social geography of cities was structured by public and private policies that encouraged consolidated black urban ghettoes while spurring white flight to suburbs. Wilder (1994) argues that the fusion of business interests with the federal Home Owners Loan Corporation (HOLC), a New Deal agency, laid the groundwork for the redlining practices of the postwar years. As part of its effort to prevent foreclosures and bank failures, the HOLC developed a "Residential Security Map" that evaluated neighborhoods, noting some as good investment areas and others as bad. According to Wilder, one of the most significant criteria for assigning a rating was the racial and ethnic composition of the residents in a community. Black communities were given the lowest ratings as were old ethnic neighborhoods with little room for new development. This system not only diminished communities with large minority populations but also devalued urban spaces in favor of undeveloped suburban ones. Over time, red lines were drawn around those neighborhoods with low ratings and banks refused to lend money to buy in them.

In the postwar years, the GI Bill (the benefits package offered to veterans of World War II) made low-interest home loans available to mostly white veterans and thus subsidized the expansion of suburbs. Redlining forced buyers to look in communities with good ratings, pushing the aspiring middle class out of cities and into suburbs. Traditional patterns of discrimination in housing and employment meant few black families had the capital to take advantage of the opportunity. Even those who had the money often were kept out of white suburbs by violence and "restrictive covenants" (statements on deeds prohibiting sale of the house to blacks). Ironically, Flatbush was given a low rating because it had too large a Jewish population, also considered a cause for concern in the 1930s. However, by the 1950s racial discourses had expanded the notion of whiteness to include Jews, enabling them to move to white suburbs (Brodkin 1998). Suburban development also required expansion of highways, water lines, and other infrastructure mostly funded with public money. Such expansion directly undermined cities by siphoning money, resources and the middle class away from them. Caught up in this web of suburbanization and "ghettoization" was Erasmus Hall, which went downhill with New York City in these years.

Beyond the policies that encouraged suburban development and discouraged investment in inner cities, older patterns of housing discrimination persisted in the postwar years. Shirley Chisholm (who represented Fort Greene in the House of Representatives in the 1970s) explained what she experienced in Brooklyn in the 1940s:

> No one knew it then, but the present-day "inner city" (to use a white euphemism) was being created. Black workers had to crowd into neighborhoods that were already black or partly so, because they could not find homes anywhere else. Buildings that had four apartments suddenly had eight, and bathrooms that had been private were shared. White building inspectors winked at housing code violations and illegal rates of occupancy, white landlords doubled and trebled their incomes on slum buildings, and the white neighborhoods in other parts of town and in the suburbs stayed white. Today's urban ghettos were being born. (1994, 50)

As white families left their neighborhoods, landlords converted their former dwellings to accommodate more and poorer families. Thus, black families were not merely replacing white families in Flatbush but were often crowding more people into subdivided spaces, increasing density. Flatbush, a working and middle-class community, had never been a slum. As more poorer and darker people moved in, slumlike conditions emerged in sections of Erasmus' encatchment area.

Not only were black families (largely Caribbean immigrants) moving into more densely crowded housing, the industrial base of Brooklyn, which had supported the dreams of the white ethnics they replaced, was deteriorating. Factories and heavy industry were also leaving Brooklyn, heading to anti-union states down south and abroad. In 1954, 235,000 people worked in manufacturing in Brooklyn. But in the 1960s, the factories began to close. Drake's Cakes, Piels, Schaefer, and Rheingold beers and machine makers of all sorts closed up shop. Between the mid-1960s and the mid-1970s two thirds of Brooklyn's manufacturing jobs had disappeared (Snyder-Grenier 1996).

The shipping industry in Brooklyn, once a major employer, was dealt its death-blow in the 1960s and 1970s as well. Shipping shifted to New Jersey, which had larger and newer facilities. The shipping industry also switched from using sacks, crates, and boxcars to large metal containers requiring one sixth the workforce to load and unload. Also, New Jersey offered easier access to the highway as trucking displaced the railroad for overland movement of goods (Snyder-Grenier 1996).

The Dodgers, the middle class, and major industry all abandoned Brooklyn between 1957 and 1977, just as newer immigrants from the Caribbean were arriving. Popular lore has tended to celebrate the struggles and triumphs of white ethnics who were able to move up and out. These popular stories do not dwell on the government assistance they had, or on what de- industrialization and the loss of so many jobs meant for the borough's residents today, and they do not focus on political and social policies that created urban ghettos and shifted precious resources away from inner cities (Brodkin 1998). The students arriving at Erasmus in the 1970s and 1980s faced very different circumstances than those who came before them: diminished employment opportunities, greater poverty, less investment in their educations, as well as the contempt of the institution and the impact of racism throughout society. Much of their struggles are left out of the narrative of decline that popularly constructs these students as agents of corrosion.

As we know from Kozol's extensive study, school funding practices that emerged in the postwar years greatly favored the rich over the poor. Particularly, they defined communities as local geographical entities (rather than regional or national entities, for example) and allowed affluent suburban communities to fund excellent schools for their children, while poorer children went unserved. Further, as the middle-class and good blue-collar jobs left cities, municipalities lost crucial tax bases and had fewer resources to invest in schools. However, beyond these economic conditions, local policies often exacerbated the problems faced by struggling urban schools. Even within urban school districts, some schools are served better than others and disturbingly, the racial composition of the school figures prominently in which schools are better resourced (Kozol 1991). In Brooklyn itself, some schools were well-maintained despite fiscal crisis while others were not.

In this essay I have sought to expand the pedagogy of place begun by Kozol in *Savage Inequalities*. Drawing on his discussion of how funding inequities create very different places for learning for rich and poor, white and black, this essay examined how these inequalities emerged historically and culturally in one school in

Brooklyn. Such an exploration reveals the ways institutionalized racism operates at a specific site. Decisions about school safety, curriculum, and how to use the campus cut black students off from the school's tradition and marginalized them both physically and academically. The steady deterioration of the physical plant and the wretched conditions that prevailed in the school further conveyed to the new students that they didn't matter. Lisette, my student from 1997, and her peers read the racism in the walls and it dampened their aspirations and limited their opportunities. It also informed them about their lesser place in American society by conveying to them visually and viscerally their diminished social standing. The narrative of decline that dominates local discourse on the school glorifies the past and derides the present, blaming decline on the students themselves. However, disinvestment in cities through deindustrialization, redlining, and subsidies to suburbs structured the racialization of space and the creation of ghetto schools. Policies and practice at the local as well as the federal level supported the decline of Erasmus Hall. Erasmus offers a story of how institutionalized racism operates to produce the savage inequalities Kozol called attention to fifteen years ago.

Notes

1. In 1898, the independent cities of Brooklyn (Kings) and Queens joined the City of New York, which comprised Manhattan, The Bronx, and Staten Island at the time. Each city became a borough and their independent school systems were also ceded to the City of New York.
2. In the mid-1970s New York fell into severe fiscal crisis and was facing bankruptcy by 1975. During these years public services were drastically cut including school budgets.
3. According to the front page of the May 16, 1969 issue of *The Dutchman* reproduced in *The Chronicles,* the Afro-American Students Association presented a list of fifteen demands to the principal and the Board of Education. Some of those demands were, "elimination of the general course of study ... end racism in hiring," and "end use of racist literature." "Teachers who are teaching a course should have a background related to the course. (No art teachers, teaching math), (No Jews teaching black history), (No Italians teaching Puerto Rican culture)." The following fall Students for a Democratic Society captured two classes by tieing up the teachers "with ropes and gags," insisting that the demands presented the previous spring be addressed. The following day three students were arrested for distributing leaflets that stated, "Yesterday a gang of white kids broke into two classes. They are part of a big gang of white kids in this country who are fighting against the pigs and for the liberation of Black people and the Vietnamese. The war is home. Which side are you on?" (235–238). These demands incorporated both the concerns raised by the Civil Rights Movement and by Black Nationalists. The disqualification of Jews and Italians to teach black and Puerto Rican culture as well as the radical attack on the general curriculum are what I am interpreting as Black Nationalist.

References

Brodkin, Karen. 1998. *How Jews Became White Folks and What That Says About Race in America.* New Brunswick, N.J.: Rutgers University Press.
Brumberg, Stephan F. 1986. *Going to America, Going to School: The Jewish Immigrant Public School Encounter in Turn-of-the-Century New York City.* New York: Praeger.

Chisholm, Shirley. 1994. "From "Unbought and Unbossed." In *The Brooklyn Reader: Thirty Writers Celebrate America's Favorite Borough*, edited by Andrea Sexton, Alice Wyatt, and Leccese Powers, 43–52. New York: Three Rivers Press.

Chronicles of Erasmus Hall High School, 1937–1987, Volume 3. 1987. New York: New York City Board of Education.

Dillon, Sam. 1993. "Years of Neglect Raise Cost of Restoring a High School: Repairs to Brooklyn's Erasmus Hall at $78 Million." *The New York Times,* 7 November, pp. 37, 44.

Gruenewald, David. 2003. "Foundations of Place: A Multidisciplinary Framework for Place-Conscious Education." *American Educational Research Journal* 40:619–654.

Hancock, Lynnell. 1992. "Halls of Shame," *New York Daily News*, February 16, 1992, pp. 1, 5, 8, 9.

Kozol, Jonathan. 1991. *Savage Inequalities: Children in America's Schools*. New York: Crown.

Lyles, Marcia V. 1992. "We Have Always Lived in the Castle: How the Politics and Culture of a School Affect Restructuring." Ph.D. dissertation, Teachers College, Columbia University.

Snyder-Grenier, Ellen. 1996. *Brooklyn! An Illustrated History.* Philadelphia: Temple University Press.

Spring, Joel. 2001. *The American School, 1642–2000.* Boston: McGraw-Hill.

Tyack, David B. 1974. *The One Best System: A History of American Urban Education.* Cambridge and London: Harvard University Press.

Tyack, David B., and Elisabeth Hansot. 1990. *Learning Together: A History of Coeducation in American Schools.* New Haven, Conn.: Yale University Press.

Waters, Mary. 1999. *Black Identities: Immigration and West Indian Dreams.* Cambridge, Mass.: Harvard University Press.

Wilder, C. S. 1994. "A Covenant With Color: Race and the History of Brooklyn, New York." Ph.D. dissertation, History, Columbia University.

Correspondence should be addressed to Maryann Dickar, Department of Teaching and Learning, New York University, 239 Greene St., New York, NY 10003. E-mail: maryann.dickar@nyu.edu

Education as a Civil Right: The Ongoing Struggle in New York

JANE FOWLER MORSE
State University of New York, Geneseo

Although New York's highest court granted children the constitutional right to a meaningful high school education in *Campaign for Fiscal Equity v. State of New York,* equitable funding has yet to be implemented. The state of New York continues to stall on revising the funding formula statewide, despite the many indications that this must be done if the state is to satisfy the Court of Appeal's 2003 ruling. Although some factors that affect children's performance in school, such as lead poisoning and poverty, lie beyond the control of the schools, schools are nevertheless required to remediate their effects by providing special education. Equitable funding based on obtaining good educational outcomes for all children would help create conditions under which children could improve their life chances through education. After equitable funding has been obtained, defining the markers of a meaningful high school education will be the next task for school reformers in New York.

Although New York's highest court granted children the constitutional right to a meaningful high school education in 2003, equitable funding has yet to be implemented. The ruling marked an enormous advance from previous interpretations of New York's constitutional requirement for a "sound basic education" to require only a minimally adequate education (New York Constitution, Article IX). The ruling may have taken place, in part, because of the Appellate Division's language in a 2002 decision, which this article explains. The failure to follow through with equitable funding, however, represents a shocking disregard for the rights of children in New York. Defining the markers of a meaningful high school education will be the next task for school reformers in New York. This article traces recent events in the case and explains why children in Rochester (and other cities) may have to initiate another court case to obtain their rights, unless the state takes action to protect its citizens without a court ruling. Fifteen years after the publication of Jonathan Kozol's (1991) powerful book, *Savage Inequalities,* the savage inequalities remain unabated in many places, including New York. Kozol graciously assumed that citizens, appalled by this situation, would fix it. More than fifteen years later, it is evident that this did not happen. Educators must become passionate advocates of social justice for children if our society is to thrive in the future.

How the Crisis in New York Arose

Publicly funded education existed in New York early in the state's history. By the twentieth century, high standards, mandated tests, Regents Examinations, and a high average per-pupil expenditure statewide became points of pride in New York. However, funding was far from equitable. Beginning in the 1920s, appointed State Commissions examined the inequities of school funding and made recommendations well into the 1970s. The most recent, the Zarb Commission (2004), referenced earlier reports by the Fleischmann (1969), Rubin (1982), Salerno (1988), and Swygert (1993) commissions, as evidence that "there has been an ongoing debate over how to improve New York's public school system. Despite the efforts of these commissions, many issues remain to be addressed today" (7). Nevertheless, the Zarb Commission (2004) congratulated New York for having one of the best public school systems in the United States. New York was among the first states to fulfill the requirements of the federal No Child Left Behind Act (NCLB). New York also has one of the highest average per-pupil expenditures in the nation. It seemed as if New Yorkers provided excellent educational opportunities to their children.

Unfortunately, the reality was otherwise for many children. The high average per-pupil expenditure masked enormous local disparities in funding (Gormley 2004). The test scores of children of poverty and children of color were, and remain, much lower than their wealthy, white, suburban counterparts. By 1973, a group of school districts brought a suit against the state for highly inequitable funding in *Levittown v. Nyquist* (1978). Although the trial court and Appellate Division ruled in favor of the plaintiff districts, the Court of Appeals ruled that the constitution did not require equitable school funding. *Levittown* judges interpreted the New York constitutional formula, requiring the state to provide all children with "a sound basic education" (New York State Constitution, Article IX), as requiring only the opportunity for a minimally adequate education, finding no unconstitutionality in a formula that presented grossly unequal disparities in funding. As judges in the Appellate Division stated, "such circumstantial findings [as lack of speech therapists, science laboratories, books, and computers] do not show that the basic educational policy of the State in marshaling an adequate foundation for its students *has been remotely violated*. It is doubtful whether cost alone is decisive of the quality of education" (emphasis mine) (*Levittown v. Nyquist* 1981, at *259). This ruling was upheld at the Court of Appeals in 1982. Following this ruling, funding gaps addressed in succeeding cases were extreme and grew wider. Deliberate public policy created and maintained a system of privilege, a caste system that was, and remains, very effective in keeping the poor in their place. Such a system, too effective to be unintentional, is not likely to be dismantled by those with a vested interest in its continuation.

Despite the fact that *Brown v. Board of Education* (1954) pronounced *de jure* segregated schools unconstitutional, and *Keyes v. School District #1* (1973) extended that to intentional, *de facto* segregated school districts, *de facto* segregation remains extreme. New York has among the most segregated suburban schools as *de facto* segregation moves to the suburbs with the exodus of middle-class people of color and immigrants (Frankenburg, Lee, and Orfield 2003; Robinson 2004). New York also has one of the highest spending gaps in the nation. When segregation and funding disparities continue without abatement over many years, it is hard to believe in the good intentions of policy makers. This caste system, starkly revealed to the public in the aftermath of Hurricane Katrina in New Orleans, has long existed and continues to exist nationwide. Intentionality also explains the political inertia following the 2003 ruling in *Campaign for Fiscal Equity v. State*.

The struggle to reform school finance in New York is not a pretty story, but one of greed, self-interest, and corruption in Albany. In the meantime, the children continue to suffer. In the long term, neglect of simple justice in school funding has resulted in racial and socioeconomic isolation of some children in illegally segregated, underfunded, decaying schools, a crass denial of the right of children to a "sound basic education." As Kozol (1991) said, "We soil them needlessly" (233).

The Campaign for Fiscal Equity Ruling

The *Levittown* (1983) ruling held that the constitution does not require equality, let alone equity. A sound basic education and "minimally adequate" facilities of learning remained the standard in New York for 30 years, not equity in spending and certainly not equality of outcomes, despite the trend in the equity movement to require adequate outcomes as opposed to equal, equitable, or even minimally adequate inputs. Not until 2003 did New York's Court of Appeals issue a ruling in favor of equality of inputs. This case, *Campaign for Fiscal Equity v. State of New York (CFE IIc)*, obtained a favorable ruling in June 2003 after six trips through the courts. The Court of Appeals remanded *Campaign for Fiscal Equity* to DeGrasse's jurisdiction after Pataki's final appeal failed, but the New York Legislature adjourned in July 2004 and again in 2005 without addressing the situation statewide. In March 2005, Justice DeGrasse denied a motion by the Campaign for Fiscal Equity organization to hold the governor and the legislature in contempt for their inaction, since the Court of Appeals had not couched its ruling as a court order. Subsequently, the New York legislature, dubbed "the most dysfunctional in the nation" by the Brennan Center for Justice of New York University, has failed to act on the ruling (Creelan and Moulton 2004). Although the state, as defendant, claims progress has been made in meeting the *CFE IIc* ruling, the trial judge, Justice LeLand DeGrasse, into whose care the case was remanded in 2003, did not agree.

In addition, endemic problems at the state level—an arcane funding formula, an entrenched bureaucracy that perpetuates the *status quo,* and a political indifference to the problems of urban, rural, poor, and minority children (who are often in the majority)—stand in the way of a statewide reform. The rights of children are not yet implemented in reality, although they have at least been given some legal status. Although the decision in *CFE IIc* grants children "a constitutional right to a meaningful high school education" specifically (*CFE IIc* at *94), the court also stated that the ruling need not apply beyond New York City (NYC) (on behalf of whose children the case was brought). It is difficult to see how children in NYC could have a constitutional right that is denied to children in the rest of the state. Meanwhile, the tyranny of the percentage rules in funding reforms. Percentage losses are moderated by the amount already in a school's budget. Stopping losses is the function of the so-called save harmless provisions in the funding formula, which sanctions this tyranny. The formula contains thirty-seven categories, many designed to benefit particular localities. Influential representation of the suburban districts in the legislature limits any catching up. It appears that if disadvantaged children must receive a meaningful high school education, then advantaged children must get something proportionately more. Maintaining the gap trumps considerations of social justice. Differences of opinion on how much is required to bring the disadvantaged children's education up to a minimal level, how much is available, and how and to whom money will be allocated are deep and bitter. The legislature saw this issue as such a political hot potato that it adjourned without addressing it in 2003, 2004, and 2005.

No Reform in 2003–2004

A charge often leveled against court-ordered school finance reform is that of judicial activism. However, people accusing the courts of taking on legislative functions must remember that courts do have the function of judicial review, vouchsafed to them by *Marbury v. Madison* in 1803 and upheld since, despite cries from conservatives of "legislating from the bench" when they don't like court decisions. The New York Legislature could implement school funding reform without a court order and the governor could propose a plan that passes constitutional muster. However, it remains the court's duty to decide whether legislative action (or inaction, in this case) is constitutional. After the state's appeal of *CFE II* failed in 2003, and after the report issued by the Special Referees appointed by DeGrasse to propose a solution in *CFE* in 2004 after the legislature failed to act, (order of the referees, September 2005), the governor proposed a restructuring that he either knew or should have known would not fulfill the court ruling or offer grounds for compromise to the democratically controlled assembly. His August 5, 2005 reply brief appealing DeGrasse's acceptance of the report of Special Referees dashed any hope of a solution for the 2005–2006 school year. The maneuvers are worthy of Jarndyce and Jarndyce in Dickens' *Bleak House*. Twelve years (and counting) have passed without a remedy in the *CFE* case, long enough for a child to have used up his or her eligibility for a sound basic education in New York, without having the resources needed to accomplish it. The NYC schools, and other schools in the state, show dropout rates that average 30 percent and test scores well below state averages. Such schools are dangerous to the children who attend them and to the society in which these children reside. Deliberate public policies of neglect and disregard for the welfare and civic competence of future citizens are disgraceful. Yet, despite the outrage of many New Yorkers and the hard work of citizen action groups, the problem remains unsolved.

In 2003, the legislature refused to act on school funding by the deadline of July 30 set by Justice DeGrasse of the trial court on *CFE*'s second trip through the courts. Governor Pataki's executive budget, devised early in the year, proposed to cut $1.24 billion from school budgets instead (Shaw 2003). Although some of these cuts were restored by the legislature in their August budget approval, schools faced a fiscal crisis of considerable proportions for the 2003–2004 school year. School budgets are planned long before August. Teachers were fired, programs cut, and inequities remained untouched. On September 3, 2003, after all parties failed to meet DeGrasse's deadline for the 2003–2004 school year, Governor Pataki appointed the Zarb Commission to examine the situation and recommend a solution. Few of the Commission's appointees came from the ranks of public education professionals. Nonetheless, the Commission agreed on many points with DeGrasse's *CFE* decision.

The Zarb Commission issued its report, titled *Ensuring Children an Opportunity for a Sound Basic Education,* on March 29, 2004. After research, which included a survey of needs done by Standard and Poor's, expert witnesses from both sides of the case, input at public meetings, and research and testimony, the governor's own commission concluded that "there are too many schools that continue to fail to provide the children with the opportunity they need to succeed" (Zarb Commission 2004, 7). The Commission "reviewed" the statewide costing-out study conducted by Campaign for Fiscal Equity during the school year 2003–2004 but preferred the methodology of Standard and Poor's, which was based on the "successful schools model," including "an efficiency factor" that consisted of selecting the expenditures of the 50 percent lowest spending successful schools as the base (which is called "the 50 percent cost reduction filter" in some documents), reasoning that the state was not required to spend above the minimal amount to provide the lowest level of adequacy (24). This model yielded a figure in the range of $2.5 billion to $5.6 billion from local, state, and federal sources combined, depending on the measure of improvement chosen, which the Commission left up to the legislature. The Commission found tax burden inequities of $11 per $1,000 in the wealthiest decile to $17.22 in the sixth decile but did not propose doing anything about these. In addition to funding, the Commission recommended a number of other reforms, including simplifying the formula from thirty-seven to eleven categories of aid; weighting expenditures for children with disabilities, children of poverty, and children who are English language learners (but different weightings than those later adopted by Degrasse's Special Referees); establishing a new, independent Office of Educational Accountability, which would use the EduStat system to track each student's progress; and others—all without any district losing any aid that it currently has. The Commission proposed that districts failing to make progress face sanctions, including closure, takeover by the state, and conversion to charter schools, which are the same sanctions that attach to failing to make adequate yearly progress (AYP) under the NCLB. In addition, the Commission proposed reforming the way building aid is disbursed and reducing the number of reports that school districts must file. To address the court's concern about unqualified teachers, the Commission proposed accelerating disciplinary hearings for teachers when loss of certification is at issue (although the Court's concern was about teachers who were not certified in the first place, not teachers who needed to be disciplined). This punitive measure does not address the need to attract and keep qualified teachers at the worst performing schools.

Following the Zarb Commission's Final Report, Governor Pataki proposed legislation that recommended allocating $1.9 billion to NYC, in an attempt to comply with the court ruling by a minimum amount. The figure he chose was significantly lower than the low end of his own commission's report. In other respects, the bill followed recommendations of the Zarb Commission, including simplifying the funding formula from thirty-seven to eleven categories, requiring districts to submit a "sound basic education" plan detailing how they planned to spend additional resources, establishing an independent Office of Educational Accountability to track the effectiveness of the additional spending, and instituting expedited measures for disciplining incompetent teachers ("Governor Vows" 2004). The democratically controlled New York Assembly opposed Pataki's choice of Standard and Poor's for the costing-out, as well as other aspects of the governor's plan. Although Senate leader Joe Bruno predicted passage of the governor's bill, the Assembly failed to agree. Despite the governor's claim to have "begun necessary and responsible action of submitting our comprehensive education reform plan to the court" ("Governor Vows" 2004), his plan proposed minimal financial improvements and imposed punitive measures that belied his claim of good intentions, although both sides agreed on some of the proposed reforms. However, the legislature remained deadlocked over the contentious issues and, in the absence of compromise, adjourned the special session without taking action. Campaign for Fiscal Equity lawyers later argued that merely proposing a remedy (which did not receive legislative approval) does not consist of compliance with the court order (Defendant's Memorandum, April 27, 2005).

No Reform in 2004–2005

In August 2004, after failure of school funding reform for the 2004–2005 school year, Justice DeGrasse appointed a three-member panel of Leo Milonas, John Feerick, and William Thompson as Special Referees to tackle the problem. The panel was charged with three tasks: (1) to ascertain the actual cost of providing a sound basic education in NYC, (2) to reform the current system of school financing to address the shortfall in NYC, and (3) to ensure a system of accountability to measure whether the reforms actually work to provide a sound basic education. The Special Referees issued their report on November 29, 2004. Their first task was to choose an appropriate costing-out methodology. In agreement with the governor's panel, they chose the "successful schools" methodology, which investigates how much it costs to replicate the results at identified successful schools. However, they disagreed with the Zarb Commission's elimination of the 50 percent highest spending schools as an efficiency factor. In his testimony to the panel, conservative Chester Finn (2004) maintained, "There is no reliable or predictable link between the resources going into a school and the learning that emerges from it" (6). Finn relied on the now-discredited Coleman Report, despite much scholarship and credible evidence to the contrary. The Special Referees did not accept this argument, as Justice DeGrasse had not in *CFE II*.

The successful schools methodology is one of three commonly identified strategies for costing-out studies; the other two are the "professional judgment" approach and the "cost estimation" approach. The Campaign for Fiscal Equity organization used the cost estimation approach to arrive at its figure of $9 billion, while school finance experts John Yinger and William Duncombe (2004) recommended a combination of approaches to arrive at their figure of $10 billion, both numbers to augment operating expenditures in NYC over four years. If the same high performance standard is chosen, Yinger and Duncombe's testimony yields similar results to those of the Campaign for Fiscal Equity organization costing-out study (and the New York State Regents independent study, which used the cost estimation model), although it is on the high side. The low end of the Standard and Poor's study was based on a lower standard than the governor's own Zarb Commission was willing to adopt. However, Governor Pataki chose a yet lower standard in recommending $1.9 billion, as the amount that the state selected "to give City students an opportunity [to receive a sound basic education]" in *CFE II* hearings, phased in over five years (rather than four) (Brief for Defendants-Appellants 2005, 2).

The standard chosen to represent adequacy matters. Yinger and Duncombe (2004) chose a high standard, measured by an index derived from test scores in math and English in third and eighth grades and high school Regents examinations. As they state, the choice of a standard is a legal/political problem, but the selection of a methodology is technical and ought to be conducted by experts. In addition, the educational consequences of teaching methods and materials are a matter of the professional judgment of educators, not bureaucrats, politicians, or economists. As Yinger and Duncombe (2004) point out, it makes no sense to penalize schools for failing to meet the standard. Punitive measures fail to examine whether the factors that contribute to the failure are inside or outside of the school's control. Yinger and Duncombe (2004) maintain that the state ought to be responsible for doing the research that enables schools to choose effective strategies and for providing adequate funding to bring the children's performance up to the chosen standard. Obviously, if the standard is set low, it will easier and less costly to implement, but Yinger and Duncombe, the Zarb Commission, the Regents, the New York Commissioner of Education, and the Campaign for Fiscal Equity organization did not recommend setting the standard low. Thus, the cost estimates ranged from a low of $2.5 billion (the low end of the Standard and Poor's Report) to a high of over $10 billion (the high end of the Yinger and Duncombe *amicus curiae* brief), for fixing the inadequacy of school finance in NYC alone. The Yinger and Duncombe brief has scholarly credibility and makes good sense but has not received the attention it deserves; the costs recommended by their combined strategies may exceed the limit of what people regard as possible. The Campaign for Fiscal Equity organization report recommended a high performance standard, but underestimated the added costs of teacher salaries and pupil disadvantages in NYC, according to Yinger and Duncombe. The Campaign for Fiscal

Equity organization's figure of $9 billion for NYC alone is not totally inconsistent with Yinger and Duncombe's results of $10 billion (phased in over four years). NYC itself asked for $5.3 billion over four years, based on Mayor Klein's *Plan of the City of New York to Provide a Sound Basic Education to all its Students,* offered in evidence to the panel of special referees on August 24, 2005. As can be seen, the governor's proposed increase of $1.9 billion fell far short of any of these amounts.

The Special Referees' second task was to recommend how to bring the funding for NYC up to constitutional levels. The Referees rejected Standard and Poor's 50 percent cost reduction filter, arguing that it does not represent efficiency and fails to take into account demographic differences, among others (Feerick, Milonas, and Thompson 2004, 16–19). They rejected the state's proposed weighting of 1.35 for pupils living in poverty, adopting a 1.5 weighting as a compromise between highs of 2.0 and lows of 1.35 from other authorities. They also updated the geographical cost index used by the state in arriving at the 1.9 billion figure. In agreement with the governor, the Special Referees adopted the Regents' Criteria for the performance measure: 80 percent of students at or above the proficiency level on state math and English Language Arts (ELA) tests at fourth grade and 80 percent of students passing five Regents' examinations, averaged over a period of at least three years. In addition, the panel recommended a capital improvement plan based on the Campaign for Fiscal Equity organization's proposal in light of the state's failure to provide an alternate plan. On this basis, the panel recommended phasing in capital improvements of $9.179 billion over five years.

In response to the third task in their charge, to implement an accountability system, the panel accepted the New York's present system of identifying Schools under Registration Review (SURR) and NCLB's requirements for AYP as adequate to provide the needed oversight without additional requirements, with enhancements agreed on by the parties, including a "Sound Basic Education Plan" (SBE Plan) to be followed by an SBE Report conducted by the State Education Department in a single, accessible document. The panel deemed a new office of Education Accountability recommended by the Zarb Commission to be redundant and costly. The three also refused to recommend changes to the state's funding formula, which was beyond their mandate. Although clearly correct by the charge given to the panel by DeGrasse, this neglect of the state's responsibility to all its children is counterproductive in the long run. Constitutional rights must be implemented statewide.

On February 14, 2005, DeGrasse accepted the Special Referee's report at the request of *CFE* lawyers, imposing a 90-day deadline for the state to implement the plan. He denied Campaign for Fiscal Equity organization's request for a citation of contempt because no "lawful judicial order expressing an unequivocal mandate" had been expressed (Index No. 111070/93, 8). DeGrasse also refused to command the state not to require the city to pay part of the amount recommended for the remedy, on the grounds that the Court of Appeals ruling stated that this is for the legislature to determine. However, the judge upheld the Special Referees' pupil weightings of 1.5 for economically disadvantaged students and their rejection of the 50 percent filter that the Zarb Commission chose to use. The panel also rejected the Zarb Commission's apparent approval of capital funding mechanisms that are in place, which included various reforms implemented by the NYC and the State Department of Education. The city's plan called for $13.2 billion, phased in over five years from 2005–2009. The Zarb Commission recommended raising the constitutional debt limit in some cases.

Governor Pataki's 2005 Executive Budget proposed increasing total school aid to $14.6 billion, which represented an increase of $147 million in general state support for public schools, again, far below amounts recommended by the Special Referees and the Zarb Commission for NYC alone. The bill added a source of funding—revenue from video lottery terminals, projected at $325 million for 2004–2005 and $2 billion annually in five years ("Governor Vows" 2004). The bill included some narrowly tailored grants, including $20.2 million dollars for Advantage Schools after-school programs (a for-profit company based in Boston), $20 million to support Teachers of Tomorrow (a program to recruit teachers for high-needs areas, which includes enticing noncertified career changers into city teaching), and $6 million for the Special Academic Improvement Program for Roosevelt School District (a Long Island school district serving a segregated population, threatened with closure for failing to make AYP under NCLB) ("Dire Options" 2000). The budget also recommended simplifying the formula statewide, changing the building aid formula, and allowing the State Dormitory Authority to oversee capital improvements—suggestions that could be helpful.

In the budget year of 2005, the New York Legislature managed to pass an on-time budget by March 31 for the first time since 1984. Education spending was increased by $848 million, but, as *The New York Times* reported, "most of the additional money [went] to districts outside New York City" (Baker 2005). Justice DeGrasse's mandate that $1.4 billion must be spent on failing city schools immediately was not heeded. According to Assemblyman Steve Sanders, the goal of passing the budget on time superseded that of complying with *CFE,* which would have required finding sources to fund increases for the city schools. Michael Rebel called the budget "flagrant contempt of the judicial branch" (Baker 2005). The legislature also failed to take action on reforming the school funding formula, according to the recommendations of the Zarb Commission. Assembly member Sam Hoyt (Democrat, Erie County) introduced a bill to create a commission "to study and make recommendations on distribution of state aid to school districts," which languishes in the Education Committee as of this writing. The legislators are also considering a bill preventing municipalities from reducing "local effort" in the eventuality that they receive more money from the state as of this writing. Assembly member Steve Sanders introduced a bill for reforming the funding in the House, but the Senate has yet to follow suit as of this writing. Ironically, in its haste to appear reformist, the New York Legislature displayed its dysfunctional nature once again, adjourning in summer of 2005 without revamping the funding formula.

The issue is further clouded by the political decision of whether to extend the solution beyond NYC. The mandate of the Special Masters extended only to the funding for NYC (Rosenberg 2004). Nonetheless, the governor's own Zarb Commission recommended statewide reforms. Without legislative support, however, their report is null. Since the governor's budget did not address the wider issue and the legislature refused to reform funding statewide, another protracted court battle may be in the offing. Utica sued for its fair share of new funding in 2004, and other cities seem likely to follow suit. Several small city school districts are suing the state for sufficient resources to provide a meaningful high school education. Regardless, Governor Pataki appealed this acceptance to the Appellate Court, First Department, asking for a stay pending appeal, to which Campaign for Fiscal Equity organization objected, asking for the stay to be denied and the appeal to be expedited (Plaintiff-Respondents' reply memorandum 2005). As of this writing, there has been no action on this appeal, and consequently no action on the *CFE* decision.

The Constitutional Right to a Meaningful High School Education

The second task for those responsible for providing a constitutional right to a sound basic education to all school children in New York is to determine an operational definition of a "meaningful high school education," in accordance with the Court of Appeals language in *CFE IIc* (2003). In 1982, the *Levittown* judges described the state constitutional obligation as minimal. The 1995 decision allowing *Campaign for Fiscal Equity* to enter its second round in the courts instructed upcoming trial judges as follows:

> Children should have access to minimally adequate instrumentalities of learning such as desks, chairs, pencils, and reasonably current textbooks. Children are also entitled to minimally adequate teaching of reasonably up-to-date basic curricula such as reading, writing, mathematics, science, and social studies, by sufficient personnel adequately trained to teach those subject areas. (*CFE/1995* at *317)

This notion of "minimally adequate" is not attractive to educators and should not be attractive to citizens either, although some argue that it is all the state requires. However, in *CFE IIa,* Justice Leland DeGrasse set forth a template that should be sufficient to direct considerable reform, even though it is not as strong as the template Kentucky judges set in *Rose*. In *CFE IIc,* the judges' statement that students in NYC have a constitutional right to a "meaningful high school education" (*CFE IIc* at *914) means that DeGrasse's template stands, since the *CFE IIc* ruling remanded the case to his court for implementation. His template includes the following seven points:

1. Sufficient numbers of qualified teachers, principals and other personnel.
2. Appropriate class sizes.

3. Adequate and accessible school buildings with sufficient space to ensure appropriate class size and implementation of a sound curriculum.
4. Sufficient and up-to-date books, supplies, libraries, educational technology and laboratories.
5. Suitable curricula, including an expanded platform of programs to help at-risk students by giving them "more time on task."
6. Adequate resources for students with extraordinary needs.
7. A safe orderly environment (*CFE IIa* at *114–5).

The Campaign for Fiscal Equity organization (2004) has recommended that a meaningful high school education contain the components mentioned in various decisions in their Sound Basic Education Task Force report. The Regents agree, clearly going beyond the idea of "minimally adequate" in their mandate to teachers in the state to accomplish the State's Learning Standards.

Despite the language in *CFE II,* on the same day, the same court argued in a second case, *Amber Paynter v. State* (2003), that the children of the Rochester City School District (RSCD) do not have a case against the state, since the plaintiffs did not argue that RSCD funding is insufficient by comparison to funding statewide, as *CFE II* established for NYC. The *Paynter* case argued that the "widespread academic failure" (not denied by anyone) caused by "racial and economic isolation" (likewise very evident) is reason for declaring the education of schoolchildren in the city of Rochester inadequate. Despite the court's decision in the case, the fact remains that these children are not receiving a meaningful high school education by any stretch of the imagination. The highly segregated city district also has a dropout rate of around 30 percent. The court in *CFE* noted that a dropout cannot be said to have received a meaningful high school education (Yinger and Dumcombe 2004). A recent Blue Ribbon Panel report, entitled "A Call to Arms," reiterates the desperate situation of the Rochester's school children (Simone et al. 2005). Likewise children in Buffalo, Yonkers, Binghamton, Syracuse, and other urban areas are not receiving a meaningful high school education by almost any standard. This issue has been raised repeatedly by the Campaign for Fiscal Equity organization and the Alliance for Quality Education, a public interest group working with Campaign for Fiscal Equity to reform the funding statewide. Furthermore, a constitutional right cannot be guaranteed in one place in the state and not in others. However, until the legislature chooses to implement a statewide solution, it is unlikely that the litigation over school finance reform in New York is over.

The concept of offering "an opportunity" for a sound basic education is problematic in the formulations of the state's obligation. In overturning Justice Degrasse's trial court ruling, the Appellate Division in *CFE IIb* implied that the children who do not take advantage of the glorious opportunity offered them in the city schools are at fault, not the schools themselves. As the judges remarked

It bears contemplation that the State's obligation is to provide children with the *opportunity* to obtain the fundamental skills comprising a sound basic education. That not all students actually achieve that level of education does not necessarily indicate a failure of the State to meet its constitutional obligations. (at *9)

The same decision declared that the old books in their libraries are "classics" (*CFE IIb* at *12), outdated computers can be used for introductory classes (*id.* at *11), and crumbling, dangerous buildings were being improved. This blatantly racist decision also stated that New York needs low-wage workers in the city, so why not be satisfied with an eighth- or ninth-grade education as the minimum standard of a sound basic education? In disputing DeGrasse, the judges commented

The term "function productively" does imply employment. It cannot be said, however, that a person who is engaged in a "low-level service job" is not a valuable, productive member of society. In reaching the contrary conclusion, the IAS court was influenced by its opinion that such jobs "frequently do not pay a living wage (*id.* at 16)." (at *8)

Somebody has to do these minimum-wage jobs, the court reasoned, and that somebody is city schoolchildren. (The same court will rule on Governor Pataki's appeal of the acceptance of the Special Referees' report.) In retrospect, public outrage against this decision may have contributed to the favorable ruling of the Court of Appeals in the final *CFE* case. However, the reasoning in this decision reared its ugly head again in the *Paynter* case, in which the Court of Appeals ruled against the Rochester plaintiffs on the very same day. If an outcome standard of adequacy determines whether or not students have received a sound, basic education, there is no way to justify the Court of Appeals' decision in *Paynter.* However, the court relied on an input measure, claiming that RSCD received its share of funding.

In an e-mail to the author in 2004, Jonathan Feldman, the lead lawyer in *Paynter,* identified the case as a desegregation case. Even though segregated schools are illegal under the 1954 *Brown* ruling, desegregation cases are no longer viable in the courts. The *Milliken v. Bradley, Board of Education v. Dowell,* and *Freeman v. Pitts* decisions have reversed the process of desegregation. In addition, many factors complicate the education of these city schoolchildren. One problem is poverty. In the deteriorating cities of New York, 25 percent to 37 percent of the children live under the poverty level with 15 percent to 20 percent of those at half the poverty level, designated to be "extreme poverty" (Children's Defense Fund). The percentages are higher for younger children. In New York's cities 25.2 percent to 44.7 percent of the children five and younger live in poverty (Children's Defense Fund). Extreme poverty amounts to $7,060 per year for a family of three. The poverty rate among children has been rising steadily since Bush took office in 2000.

The reported rate in 2003 was the highest it has been since 1980 (Dillon 2003). Further increases were recorded in 2004 (U.S. Census Bureau 2005).

Another factor is lead poisoning, a big problem in Rochester, since the housing stock is old, wooden, and deteriorating. Still widespread in some places, lead poisoning is a problem that has yet to be solved. Although this is outside the control of schools, schools nevertheless compensate for it. Special education, because of its federal mandate, represents a major factor in the expenses incurred by city schools. It can cost up to three or four times what regular education costs. In "Where's the Money Going?," Richard Rothstein (1997) points out that the cost of regular education has been steadily shrinking as the cost of federally mandated special education rises. Conservatives like Finn do not take this into account when they cite increases in school spending that do not result in increased test scores. Many of these costs are directly linked to lead poisoning. When children are damaged by lead, it is unfair to say that they are failing to take advantage of the opportunity for a sound basic education that is so graciously offered to them. Although the cost of cleaning up lead in the housing stock is high by some standards, it nevertheless surely makes more sense to stop poisoning children in the first place than it does to remedy the effects (albeit ineffectively) with special education. Lead damage is permanent. When the cost of the lifetime effects of lead poisoning are calculated, abatement proves to be much cheaper than special education, unemployment, crime, and incarceration. In addition, the waste of human potential is incalculable. Ignoring such conditions is not only imprudent, but also immoral.

The connection between lead poisoning and crime is becoming clearer to social scientists, despite a shortage of data pertinent to this point. Children on Medicaid in New York are not screened for lead. In nearby Rhode Island, only one fifth of children on Medicare were screened for lead, according to a Government Accounting Office report (Vivier at al. 2001). Patrick Vivier and his coauthors report that of those tested, 29 percent had a blood lead level of more than or equal to 10 mg/dL (the currently "safe" level is 10 mg/dL, despite evidence that any level of lead is unsafe). Blood lead levels vary by many factors, including type of primary care provider site, race/ethnicity, language spoken at home, parental education, and location of residence. In particular, the race/ethnicity factor is strong. The prevalence of lead poisoning in Rhode Island is 23.5 percent for white, 41.3 percent for black, 26.7 percent for Hispanic, and 53.9 percent for other. Urban children are especially affected; 31.4 percent of urban children are poisoned, as compared to 18.8 percent in other areas. In addition, 45 million people in the United States currently lack health care coverage (U.S. Census Bureau 2005). Their children are less likely to be screened, which provides an underestimation of the prevalence of lead poisoning among the poor.

The connection of lead poisoning with many other problems is documented (Trope, Lopez-Villegas, Cecil, and Lenkinski 2001). Many poor children suffer from lead poisoning that reduces their IQ (Lanphear et al. 2000); increases antisocial behavior and aggression ("Lead Exposure " 2003) and school failure; and is even correlated to tooth decay, retarded growth ("Effects" 1991; Moss et al. 1999), and delays in the development of puberty in girls (Selevan et al. 2003). Herbert Needleman et al. (2002) reported that adjudicated juveniles living in Pittsburg had four times the bone lead levels as their matched, non-adjudicated peers. A 2004 study shows a positive correlation between elevated air-lead levels and both violent and property crime (Stretesky and Lynch 2004). However, President Bush rejected Dr. Bruce Lanphear, whose research shows that any level of lead is harmful, after he was nominated by Clinton to serve on the Centers for Disease Control and Prevention committee that reviews lead poisoning. The committee was stacked instead with known pro-lead industry members. Other problems plague children of the poor lack of health care, poor nutrition, lack of safe surroundings, lack of quality daycare, homelessness, dental problems, and many more. Schools do not cause these conditions but could ameliorate them at far less cost and with far greater humanity than programs that deal with the aftermath of a lack of education.

Failure to Provide a Meaningful High School Education in Rochester

Because of the complex mix of the factors cited previously, children in Rochester require more expenditure per pupil to educate than suburban children. However, the racial and economic isolation that provided the basis of the law case is a major factor. It is fairly well known that such isolation magnifies its ill effects. Parents in Rochester have been fighting inadequate education since 1999 when the Greater Rochester Area Coalition for Education brought the initial suit against the RSCD in *Amber Paynter v. State [Paynter Ia]*. In a complicated series of maneuvers, the trial court dismissed part of the charges in November 2000, requiring the plaintiffs to join the suburban districts to the defendants, despite their reluctance to do so because the suburban districts had done nothing wrong. However, the court insisted, since they would be involved in any remedy. At the Appellate Division in *Paynter Ib* in December 2001, the court dismissed the remainder of the charges, including those against the suburban districts. Only Judge J. P. Green dissented in part. He agreed that the charges against the suburban school districts were properly dismissed but disagreed with the dismissal of the civil rights charges. He held that wholesale academic failure merited a trial to determine whether children in Rochester had the opportunity of a sound basic education. In *Paynter Ib,* he stated, plaintiffs are "alleging that they are deprived of this constitutional right [to a sound basic education] as a result of causes unrelated to funding" (*Paynter Ib* at *106). Judge Green suggested that the state, through its regulations about housing and school attendance zones, might indeed be responsible. He pointed out that the majority inappropriately concluded that "there will be myriad reasons for academic failure that are beyond the control of the State before the plaintiffs had an opportunity to make their case" (at *107). This ruling preceded DeGrasse's decision in Campaign for Fiscal Equity (*CFE IIa*) by two weeks, but Green was a minority of one. Now it was the plaintiffs' turn to appeal. At this point, the United States Supreme Court ruled in *Alexander v Sandoval* (2001) that individuals do not have a right to sue under the 1964 Civil Rights Act, undoing 40 years of protection against disparate impact discrimination. This case took its toll on *Paynter.*

The plaintiffs appealed to the Court of Appeals and the case was heard on the same day, by the same court, as the *CFE* case. Unfortunately, *Paynter Ic* case failed because, as the court said, plaintiffs could not claim that the district was underfunded. Despite their pronouncement in *CFE* that children had a right to a meaningful high school education in NYC, the court refused a remedy for the harms done to Rochester's schoolchildren, falling back on the claim that the causes lie outside the control of the schools. However, the schools are both *compelled* to remedy those harms (through special education which is mandated by the federal government) and *in a position* to remedy these harms. New York schools are all required to provide a meaningful high school education. They are specifically enjoined from claiming that the "opportunity" was provided when a high dropout rate and abysmally low test scores persist. The "widespread academic failure" alleged by the *Paynter* case was not under any dispute. Nor was the contention that it was caused by economic and racial isolation. The court ignored the fact that segregated school districts, which are created by the state's rules, impose the racial and economic isolation that results in Rochester's failure in the first place. By law, the city school district lines must be coterminous with the city's boundaries, city schoolchildren must attend in their district of residence, and low income housing cannot be built in the suburbs without the consent of suburban residents, which they often do not give. Consequently, public housing is concentrated in the city. The state is also responsible for failure to enforce Housing and Urban Development rules concerning lead-safe housing, the failure to provide lead-safe low income housing, and the failure to hold landlords or realtors responsible for locating poor families in unsafe housing. The burden of proof is on the family, which must show that the landlord knew that the housing was unsafe and had an opportunity to remodel it (when, presumably, the family would be living elsewhere at their own expense during remodeling while continuing to pay rent) (see *Chapman v. Silber* 2001).

In addition, the latest funding decisions rely on an adequacy standard, rather than a standard based on the level of funding. The Court in *Paynter Ic* relied instead on an input standard—the amount of money expended per pupil. An adequacy standard is an output standard. Academic outputs must be adequate, rather than the inputs being equal, or even equitable. It will matter how the standard of adequacy is set and how it is measured, but the *CFE* decision made it clear that children must be accorded an education that allows them to develop civic competence and compete in the labor market. *CFE IIc* added that a meaningful high school education is a civil right in New York. Although the *CFE* decision does not allow the Regents' Learning Standards alone to be the definition of a meaningful high school education, nevertheless, DeGrasse's template stands. The children in Rochester cannot be said to have access to an education meeting DeGrasse's template.

Conclusion: What New York (and Other States) Could Do

Given these factors, what are the schools to do? Citizens, both those with a social conscience and those concerned mainly with their taxes, ought to be outraged that the root causes of school failure remain unaddressed—lead poisoning, poverty, ill health, unemployment or underemployment, incarceration, and more. It makes no sense, from a humanitarian or from a policy point of view, to remediate these effects when the state could prevent them. However, right now, city schools need more money because of the added costs of educating of lead-poisoned, impoverished, malnourished, ill children in special education classes. In addition to lead poisoning, other factors hinder the accomplishment of a meaningful high school education in New York—lack of medical care, extreme poverty, extreme segregation by race and socioeconomic status, environmental toxins, and more. Although the state technically may not be responsible for these factors, the state is in a position to do something about them. State and local laws can mandate lead-safe housing, provide medical care and lead screening, implement a living wage policy, provide early childhood education, raise the earned income tax credits, and fund many more programs known to work (Blank 1997). The state also can cease to isolate children of color and children of poverty in city schools. Such isolation is known to be harmful.

Aristotle's *Politics* contains the earliest notion of social justice. Aristotle claims that the purpose of much of justice is rectifying wrongs done. When wrongs are permitted by the state, the state should be responsible for righting them. Many of the factors harming children's performance in school that I have examined in this article are things should be addressed by the state. Although education alone cannot remedy every factor that affects children's performance in schools, it is certainly in the position to remedy those in which it is complicit. Public education is an appropriate vehicle for the state to use to remediate social injustices. As long as factors impede the education of children, education spending will be pressed to accommodate their needs. A top-notch education for NYC schoolchildren, according to Yinger and Duncombe (2004), would cost $20,000 per-pupil expenditure in the city for the thirteen years of school age (or maybe fifteen if we add preschool). Expensive as this is, incarceration costs more. Keeping an inmate in prison can cost double and triple the price tag of an excellent education. A mandatory sentence of fifteen years to life for minor drug crimes exceeds a child's eligibility for school services. The New York Legislature has yet to reform the Rockefeller drug laws, which mandate punishment rather than treatment ("Drop the Rock" n.d.). Other hidden costs include lost income in the cycle of underemployment and unemployment following incarceration, loss of parental presence for young children, and loss of civility in society. In the United States, incarceration has soared since the 1980s, making the United States first in the world in incarceration rates, with over 2.2 million prisoners. Few of these prisoners vote while imprisoned, and many of them lose the franchise for life. Prison becomes the holding pen for under-educated, functionally illiterate citizens. Meanwhile, New York spends more money on prisons than on higher education. Surely it would make more sense to in-vest money in lead abatement, education, decent and meaningful employment, medical care for children and their parents, nutrition programs, and reforms to re-duce poverty. President Lyndon Johnson's War on Poverty was successful in re-ducing the income gap in the 1970s. The work of Rebecca M. Blank (1997) and the Milton S. Eisenhower Foundation's report, *The Millennium Breach* (1998) show that many other programs work to reduce poverty—food stamps, nutritional sup-port for women and children, Section 8 housing vouchers for low income housing in the suburbs, job training, earned income tax credits, early childhood education, and more. They are relatively inexpensive compared to the cost of the war on Iraq, the incarceration of our citizens, the destructive effects of poverty on our children, the high cost of special education, crime, lead poisoning, and more. An excellent education can help children overcome conditions that lead to the perpetuation of poverty and despair.

New York's recent history shows massive disregard for social justice in school funding. The *CFE IIc* ruling should have resulted in some correction, at least for NYC. Despite this, nothing much has happened yet. In his writings, Kozol contin-ues to reveal the pain and sorrow that social injustice places on the lives of real children, many of them living in New York. Ordinary people should be outraged at the suffering his work reveals. Maybe reform of school funding will be forthcom-ing in New York, but the fight seems interminable, with the state resisting every inch of the way. When reforms are finally enacted, they will be a tribute to the com-passion of Kozol and the persistence of school funding reformers who have been pursuing social justice for the children of New York for over thirty years. The story is not over yet, but I hope the final chapter is about to be written.

References

Cases

Alexander v. Sandoval (Sandoval), Individually and ex rel all others similarly situated, No. 99-1908, 2001 U.S. LEXIS 3367 (U.S. April 24, 2001).
Board of Educ. v. Dowell, No. 89 080, 1991 U.S. LEXIS 484 (U.S. January 15, 1991).
Brown v. Board of Education (Brown I), No. 1, 1954 U.S. LEXIS 2094, at * 495 (U.S. May 17, 1954).
Campaign for Fiscal Equity v. New York (CFE/1995), No. 117A, 1995 N.Y. LEXIS 1145 (N.Y. June 15, 1995).

Campaign for Fiscal Equity (CFI IIa) v. State, No. 111070/93, 2001 N.Y. Misc. LEXIS 1 (N.Y. Sup. Ct., N.Y. Co., January 9, 2001).

Campaign for Fiscal Equity, Inc. (CFE IIb) v. New York, No. 5330, 2002 N.Y. App. Div. LEXIS 7252 (N.Y. App. Div. June 25, 2002).

Campaign for Fiscal Equity, Inc. (CFE IIc), Respondents v. State of New York et al., Appellants, No. 74, The Court of Appeals of New York, 2003, LEXIS N.Y. 1678.

Chapman v. Silber; Stover v. Robilotto, No. 128, No. 129, The Court of Appeals of New York, N.Y. LEXIS 3408. (November 15, 2001).

Freeman v. Pitts, No. 89-1290, 1992 U.S. LEXIS 2114 (U.S. March 31, 1992).

Keyes v. Sch. Dist. #1, No. 71-507, 1973 U.S. LEXIS 43 (U.S. June 21, 1973).

Levittown v. Nyquist (1978), 94 Misc. 2d. LEXIS 2270.

Levittown v. Nyquist (1981), 83 A.D.2d 217, LEXIS 14777.

Levittown v. Nyquist (1982), 57 N.Y.2d 27, LEXIS 3535.

Levittown Board of Educ. v. Nyquist, No. 82 39; No. 82 55, 1983 U.S. LEXIS 3048 (U.S. Jan. 17, 1983).

Marbury v. Madison (1803), 5 U.S. 137; LEXIS 352.

Milliken v. Bradley (Milliken I), No. 73 34, 1974 U.S. LEXIS 94 (U.S. July 25, 1974).

Paynter, Individually and ex rel All Others Similarly Situated [Paynter Ia], No. 98/10280, 2000 N.Y. Misc. LEXIS 569 (N.Y. Sup. Ct. Nov. 14, 2000).

(Stone ex rel) Paynter (Paynter, Appellate Division), *and ex re All Others Similarly Situated v. New York [Paynter Ib],* No. (232), CA 99 24, 2000 N.Y. App. Div. LEXIS 3626, at *820 (N.Y. App. Div. March 29, 2000).

(Stone ex rel.) Paynter (Paynter, Court of Appeals) *v. New York [Paynter Ic],* No. 75, 2003 N.Y. LEXIS 1672 (N.Y. June 26, 2003).

Motions and Other Legal Documents

Defendants' memorandum in opposition to plaintiff's motion to vacate automatic stay. (April 27, 2005). Supreme Court of the State of New York Appellate Division: First Department. Index No. 111070/93. http://www.cfequity.org

DeGrasse, Justice Leland. (February 14, 2005). No title. Document accepting plaintiff's motion to accept Referees' report; rejecting Defendant-respondent's motion to reject the Referees' report; and rejecting plaintiffs' motion to punish defendants with civil contempt. Supreme Court of the State of New York County of New York. Index No. 111070/93. http://www.cfequity.org

———. Notice of Entry. (Accepting Report of Referees) (March 22, 2005) Supreme Court of the State of New York County of New York. Index No. 111070/93. http://www.cfequity.org

Brief for Defendants-Appellants. (August 5, 2005). Supreme Court of the State of New York Appellate Division: First Department. Index No. 111070/93. http://www.cfequity. org

Brief for Plaintiffs-Respondents. (September 7, 2005). Supreme Court of the State of New York Appellate Division: First Department. Index No. 111070/93. http://www.cfequity. org

Feerick, John D., E. Leo Milonas, and William C. Thompson. (November 30, 2004). Report and Recommendations of the Judicial Referees. Supreme Court of the State of New York County of New York: IAS Part 25. Index No. 111070/93. http://www.cfequity.org

———. Order of the Referees. (September 2005). Supreme Court of the State of New York Appellate Division: First Department. Index No. 111070/93. http:// www.cfequity.org

Plaintiff-Respondents' reply memorandum of law in support of their motion to vacate the statutory stay and to expedite the appeal. (April 28, 2005). Supreme Court of the State of New York Appellate Division: First Department. Index No. 111070/93. http://www. cfequity.org

Other Text References

Baker, Al. 2005. "Albany Passes the Budget on Time; A First Since '84." *The New York Times,* April 1. *LexisNexis News.*

Blank, Rebecca M. 1997. *It Takes a Nation: A New Agenda for Fighting Poverty.* The Russell Sage Foundation. Princeton, N.J.: Princeton University Press.

Brennan Center for Justice, New York University School of Law. 2004. *New Report: New York's Legislative Process Most Dysfunctional in Nation.* http:// www.brennancenter. org/presscenter/releases_2004/

Campaign for Fiscal Equity. 2004. *Sound Basic Education Task Force: Ensuring Educational Opportunity For All,* April 22. http://www.cfequity.org

Children's Defense Fund. n.d. *Children in New York in Poverty.* http://www. cdfny.org/ RR/CDFdata.htm

Creelan, Jeremy M., and Laura M. Moulton. 2004. *The New York State Legislative Process: An Evaluation and Blueprint for Reform.* http://www.brennancenter.org/presscenter/ releases_2004/

Dillon, Sam. 2003. "Report Finds Number of Black Children in Deep Poverty Rising." *The New York Times,* April 30. *LexisNexis News.*

"Dire Options Debated for Roosevelt School: State Will Watch Student Performance this Year at Long Island School." 2000. *The New York Teacher,* September 27. http://www. nysut.org/newyorkteacher/2000–2001/000927roosevelt.html

"Drop The Rock: The Campaign to Repeal the Rockefeller Drug Laws." n.d. http://www. droptherock.org/DTR_Talking_Pts_with_graphics.htm

"Effects of Blood Lead Level on Growth." 1991. *Nutrition Research Newsletter* 10 (9): 88.

Finn, Chester. 2004. Testimony, October 1. www.cfequity.org/FinnTestimony.pdf

Frankenburg, Erica, Chungmei Lee, and Gary Orfield. 2003. *A Multiracial Society with Segregated Schools: Are We Losing the Dream?* www.civilrightsproject.harvard.edu/research/ reseg03/resegregation03.php

Gormley, Michael. 2004. "Study, NY School Funding Gap One of Biggest in the Nation." Associated Press State and Local Wire, Oct. 6. *LexisNexis News.*

"Governor Vows Not to Give Up; Will Continue Fight to Ensure that Every Child in New York Receives the Quality Education They [sic] Deserve." 2004. Governor Press Release, July 30. http://www.ny.gov/governor/press/05/index_d. html

Klein, Mayor Joel. 2005. *Plan of the City of New York to Provide a Sound Basic Education to All Its Students,* offered in evidence to the panel of special referees on August 24. http://www.cfequity.org

Kozol, Jonathan. 1991. *Savage Inequalities: Children in America's Schools.* New York: Crown.

Lanphear, Bruce J., Kim Deitrich, Peggy Auinger, and Christopher Cox. 2000. "Cognitive Deficits Associated with Blood Lead Concentrations < 10 Micrograms per Deciliter in US Children and Adults. U.S. Department of Health and Human Services. 2000. *Public Health Reports* 115:521–529.

"Lead Exposure and Behavior." 2003. *Pediatrics for Parents* 19: 12 (Feb. 2): n.p.

Moss, Mark E., Bruce P. Lanphear, and Peggy Auinger. 1999. "Association of Dental Caries and Blood Lead Levels." *Journal of the American Medical Association* 281 (24): 2294.

Needleman, Herbert L., Christine McFarland, Roberta B. Ness, Stephen E. Fienberg, Michael J. Tobin. 2002. "Bone Lead Levels in Adjudicated Delinquents: A Case Control Story." *Neurotoxicology and Teratology* 24:711–717.

New York State Constitution. http://www.yale.edu/lawweb/avalon/states/ ny01.htm

Robinson, Gail. 2004. "New York Schools: Fifty Years After Brown." *Gotham City Gazette: New York City News and Policy,* May 17. http://www.gothamgazette. com/article/ 20040517/200/981

Rothstein, Richard. 1997. "Where's the Money Going?" Economic Policy Institute, November. http://www.epinet.org/content.cfm/books_wheremoneyes

Rosenberg, Erika. 2004. "Trio Takes Over Revamp of Aid." *Rochester Democrat and Chronicle,* August 4. http://www.rochesterdandc.com/news/forprint/ 0804NM54EGJ_news.shtml

Selevan, Sherry G., Deborah C. Rice, Karen A. Hogan, Susan Y. Euling, et al. 2003. "Blood Lead Concentration and Delayed Puberty in Girls." *New England Journal of Medicine* 348:1527–1536. http://www.ncbi.nlm.nih.gov/entrez/query.fcgi?cmd=Retrieveanddb=Pub Medandlist_uids=1270 0372anddopt=Abstract

Shaw, Elliott. 2003. Summary of the Governor's Proposed 2003–2004 Budget, The Business Council of New York. January 31. http://www.bcnys.org/inside/gac/BUDSUM0304.htm

Simone, Albert J., et al. 2005. *Call to Arms: Report of the Blue Ribbon Task Force to Assess the Rochester City School District's Financial Practices and their Relationship to Educational Outcomes,* August. www.rit.edu/~020www/docs/ **blue**RibReport_8–05.pdf

Stretesky, Paul B., and Michael J. Lynch. 2004. "The Relationship Between Lead and Crime." *Journal of Health and Social Behavior* 45 (June): 214–229.

The Milton S. Eisenhower Foundation. 1998. *The Millenium Breach: The American Dilemma, Richer and Poorer.* http://www.eisenhowerfoundation.org/aboutus/fr_publications.html

Trope, Idit, Dolores Lopez-Villegas, Kim M. Cecil, and Robert E. Lenkinski. 2001. "Exposure to Lead Appears to Selectively Alter Metabolism of Cortical Gray Matter." *Pediatrics* 107:1437–1443.

U.S. Census Bureau. 2005. Press Release CB05-125, "Income Stable, Poverty Rate Increases, Percentage of Americans Without Health Insurance Unchanged." August 30. http://www.census.gov/Press-Release/www/releases/archives/income_wealth/005647.html

Vivier, Patrick M., Joseph W. Hogan, Peter Simon, Tricia Leddy, Lynne M. Dansereau, and Anthony J. Alerio. 2001. "A Statewide Assessment of Lead Screening Histories of Preschool Children Enrolled in a Medicaid Managed Care Program." *Pediatrics* 108:458.

Yinger, John, and William Duncombe. 2004. Amicus Curiae Brief. September 17. http://crp.maxwell.syr.edu/pbriefs/pb28.pdf

Zarb Commission, Frank E. Zarb, Chairman. 2004. *The New York State Commission on Education Reform: Ensuring Children An Opportunity for a Sound Basic Education, Final Report.* March 29. http://www.state.ny.us/pdfs/finalreportweb.pdf

Correspondence should be addressed to Jane Fowler Morse, School of Education, SUNY, Geneseo, 1 College Circle, Geneseo, NY 14454. E-mail: jfmorse@geneseo.edu

Savage Inequalities Revisited: Adequacy, Equity, and State High Court Decisions

DEBORAH A. VERSTEGEN
University of Nevada

KRISTAN VENEGAS
University of Nevada

ROBERT KNOEPPEL
University of Kentucky

Skye Morgan will enter Alaska's Aniak elementary school in two to three years.[1] The school she will enter has no instruction in science, foreign languages, art, instrumental music, vocal music, or physical education. When she moves to high school she will not have an opportunity to take advanced placement classes, biology, geography, political science, world languages, English (debate, drama, journalism, speech), or a variety of other courses. The school district she will enter is not accredited and is on the list of "failed schools" by the Alaska Department of Education. Virtually every student has special needs and the district has one of the highest proportions of students who are Alaska Natives, have limited English proficiency, and are living in poverty. More than 50 percent of Skye's peers in the Aniak schools are not proficient in reading, writing, or arithmetic; 70 percent of the tenth, eleventh, and twelfth grade students are not proficient in writing, 80 percent are not proficient in reading, and 90 percent are not proficient in math.

Skye will begin school with the deck stacked against her ability to succeed academically and beat the system. However, we must ask, should Skye and other innocent children like her be faced with that difficult test so early in their lives—one that likely will place them at risk for graduation and a decent job, competition for college entrance, or even full participation in our democratic system of government? They are, after all, children. They cannot go down to city hall and register a complaint, advocate for increases in taxes to fund necessary school classes, or participate in legislative hearings on the very issues that plague the schools in which they will spend at least twelve years during the most formative time of their lives.

On behalf of children like Skye, parents recently have joined with others to challenge not just the desirability but the constitutionality of state funding systems that result in what Jonathan Kozol (1991) has called the "savage inequalities" in our nation's schools. Since *Savage Inequalities* was written, however, another issue has become prominent: adequacy. Unlike an equity claim that may apply only to poor districts within a state, an adequacy challenge can apply to an entire state system of education. This gives credence to the notion of savage inadequacies, where an equality of poverty may prevail across the state and all children—rich and poor alike—are disadvantaged by an underfunded, insufficient, and unsatisfactory educational system. In fact, the recent complaint from Alaska alleges that "*Every* Alaskan child receives an inadequate education because the funding of that education is grossly inadequate" (emphasis added) (Kristine Moore v. State of Alaska).

State high court decisions on the constitutionality of state school funding systems have highlighted factual evidence related to state funding, constitutional history, and other state contextual factors that result in diminished opportunities and outcomes for all children but particularly children of color, the poor, non-Native English speakers, and students with special needs. The evidence presented in this "new wave" of school finance litigation focuses directly on adequacy in the level of educational opportunities offered to school children in one or more schools and districts within a state and shows that some students are not receiving a sufficient education as required under the constitution and as measured by contemporary education standards, by state rules and regulations, and/or by comparisons to other school systems or states (Verstegen 1994). Thus, in assessing the constitutionality of the finance system, courts have shifted their focus, moving to include disparities in substantive education content in addition to dollars and other educational input and output factors. In essence, courts are interested in determining whether a certain quality of education is available to all children and are looking at disparities not only in terms of dollars but also in terms of what dollars buy—including teachers, class sizes, technology, materials, curriculum, facilities, and budget flexibility (Verstegen 2002, 2004a, 2004b). Do savage inequalities still exist? A review of state high court opinions on the constitutionality of the education funding system issued since the release of Kozol's book suggest the answer is "yes."

High Court Challenges to State Education Systems

Issues of adequacy and equity are highlighted in the landmark Kentucky case, *Rose v. Council for Better Education, Inc.* (1989). The high court dramatically extended the reach of school finance litigation and found the entire education system, not just the finance system, unconstitutional, including the statutes creating, implementing, governing, and financing the system and all regulations. Experts testified that "without exception, there is great disparity among poor and wealthy districts in Kentucky regarding basic educational materials; student-teacher ratios; curriculum; size, adequacy and condition of physical plant; and quality of basic management." They found "a definite correlation between the amount of money spent per child on education and the quality of education received—which was corroborated by evidence." Variations among poor and rich districts were found in finances, taxable property, curriculum (especially foreign language, science, mathematics, music and art), test scores, and student-teacher ratios. Not only did poorer districts provide an inadequate education, when judged by "accepted national standards," affluent districts' efforts were found to be inadequate as well (*Rose v. Council for Better Education, Inc.* 1989).

Comparisons of Kentucky with adjacent states—Ohio, Indiana, Illinois, Missouri, Tennessee, Virginia, and West Virginia—included rankings on per-pupil expenditures, average annual salary of instructional staff, classroom teacher compensation, property tax revenue as a percentage of total revenue, percentage of ninth-grade students graduating from high school, pupil-teacher ratios, and ACT scholastic achievement test scores. The data showed Kentucky ranked nationally in the lower 20 percent to 25 percent in virtually every category used to evaluate educational performance and did not provide uniform opportunities among school districts. Thus, the high court found the system inadequate and unconstitutional for all districts, both rich and poor alike.[2]

Likewise in Montana, the high court struck down the finance system based on the "plain" meaning of the education article, after reviewing it to determine whether all children had equal access to a quality education—not a basic or minimum education. The court found the system inadequate to meet this task, noting that the accreditation standards provided only a "minimum upon which a quality education can be built." Comparisons of similarly sized high- and low-spending school districts showed advantages for high-spending districts such as "greater budget flexibility to address educational needs and goals" in addition to enriched and expanded curricula, better equipped schools in terms of textbooks, instructional equipment, audio-visual instructional materials, consumable materials and supplies, computer labs, libraries, and better facilities. The evidence demonstrated that the "wealthier school districts are not funding frills" and disparities cannot be described as the result of local control. In fact, the present system "may be said to deny to poorer school districts a significant level of local control, because they have fewer options due to fewer resources" (*Helena Elementary School District v. State* 1989).

In Texas, the high court thrice invalidated the system in less than 28 months; additional decisions followed. In the initial *Edgewood* 1989 decision, the court pointed out the gross disparities that existed among school districts in the state and found that educational programs in poor districts were not only inferior to those in wealthy districts but in many cases did not even meet minimum state standards. For example, San Elizario Independent School District offered no foreign language, no prekindergarten program, no chemistry, no physics, no calculus, and no college preparatory or honors program. Extracurricular programs were almost nonexistent. There was no band, debate, or football. On the other hand, the court said:

> High wealth districts are able to provide for their students broader educational
> experiences including more extensive curricula, more up-to-date technological

equipment, better libraries and library personnel, teacher aides, counseling services, lower student-teacher ratios, better facilities, parental involvement programs, and drop-out prevention programs. They are also better able to attract
and retain experienced teachers and administrators. (*Edgewood* 1989)

Another high court decision is expected in the long saga of funding equity and adequacy in the state of Texas.

In New Jersey the *Abbott* court has struck down the finance system more than
seven times since 1985—not in total, but for 30 poorer urban districts.[3] In the second ruling (*Abbott II*) the court noted that poorer urban districts, in contrast to
more affluent localities, had inferior course offerings, dilapidated facilities, greater
student needs, higher drop-out rates, lower educational expenditures, and failing
scores on the High School Equivalency Test. The high court found that the poorer
the district, the greater its need, the less the money available, and the worse the education. The New Jersey court held that a thorough and efficient education means
more than teaching the basic skills needed to compete in the labor market, although
this is important. A thorough and efficient education would enable all students to
fulfill their role as a citizen; to participate fully in society and in the life of their
community; and to appreciate art, music, and literature. As the court said:

> If absolute equality were the constitutional mandate, and "basic skills" suffi-
> cient to achieve that mandate, there would be little short of a revolution in the
> suburban districts when parents learned that basic skills is what their children
> were entitled to, limited to, and no more. (*Abbott II*)

The opinion cited disparities in education curricula that were linked to local district wealth and spending. For instance, affluent Princeton had one computer per
eight children while poor Camden had one computer per fifty-eight children.
Princeton had seven science laboratories in its high school, each with built-in
equipment, but some poor urban districts offered science in labs built in the 1920s
or 1930s. Others provided no lab experience at all or wheeled science materials
around the school on a cart to furnish supplies. Montclair's students began instruction in French or Spanish at the preschool level. In Princeton's four-year high
school, programs were also available in German, Italian, Russian, and Latin in addition to advanced placement courses. However, many poorer schools did not even
offer upper-level foreign language courses, and only limited courses were available in high school.

Wealthy South Brunswick offered music classes starting in kindergarten. Montclair began with preschoolers and every elementary school had an art classroom
and art teacher. In contrast, poor Camden eliminated all of its elementary school
music teachers and could only provide "helpers" to teach art. Another poor urban

school provided an art room in the back of the lunchroom, and there were no art classrooms at all in East Orange elementary schools.

Many richer suburban school districts had flourishing gymnastics, swimming, basketball, baseball, soccer, lacrosse, field hockey, tennis, and golf teams with fields, courts, pools, lockers, showers, and gymnasiums, but in East Orange the track team practiced in the second floor hallway, and there were no sports facilities. Irvington's elementary schools did not have outdoor play space. Facilities in poor urban districts were often in disrepair, overcrowded, unsafe, and threatened the safety of children. For example, in East Orange, thirteen schools needed asbestos removal or containment, thirteen required structural system repairs, and fifteen had heating, ventilation, or air conditioning problems. Moreover, poor urban districts were crowded. In Paterson children ate lunch in a small area in the boiler room of the basement. Remedial classes were taught in a former bathroom. A school in East Orange had no cafeteria, so the children ate lunch in shifts in the first-floor corridor, and a class was held in a converted coal bin. Thus, the high court ordered funding parity between poor urban and wealthy suburban districts with additional funds for the special needs of urban school children in the Abbott districts.

In the 1997 decision (*Abbott IV*) the court underscored the importance of sufficient funding, again ordering parity between poor urban and wealthy suburban districts in addition to a study of the supplemental programmatic and facilities needs of urban schools. The Comprehensive Education Improvement and Financing Act, enacted in 1996 to address the issues, the court said,

> failed to address the estimated "$6 billion" in facility needs .... Such a failure
> is of constitutional significance—we cannot expect disadvantaged children to
> achieve when they are relegated to buildings that are unsafe and often incapable
> of housing the very programs needed to educate them.[4]

The New Jersey high court also ordered a full complement of "supplemental programs ... to wipe out disadvantages as much as a school can," including well planned, high-quality preschool education for all three- and four-year-old children in the Abbott districts. These must be adequately funded by the state, the court declared (*Abbott IV* and *Abbott V*).

The Tennessee high court, finding inadequacy and inequity in the school finance system, invalidated the finance plan citing testimony that schools in poorer districts often have "decaying physical plants, some school buildings are not adequately heated," and textbooks and libraries are "inadequate, outdated, and in disrepair." Lack of funds prevented poor schools from offering advanced placement courses, more than one foreign language at a high school, state-mandated art and music classes, drama instruction, and extracurricular athletic teams. Some schools did not provide adequate science laboratories, and "the teachers buy supplies with their own money to stock the labs," or "schools engage in almost constant fundrais-ing by students to provide the needed materials" (*Tennessee Small Sch. Sys. v. McWherter* 1993).

In wealthier Tennessee school districts, 66 percent of the elementary schools and 77 percent of the secondary schools were accredited compared to only 7 per-cent and 40 percent among the ten poorest districts. "All of the schools in [wealthy] Kingsport and Shelby County districts were accredited. In contrast, none of the [poor districts in] Clay County, Wayne County, Hancock County and Crockett County schools were accredited." Students attending the unaccredited schools have a higher need for remedial courses at college, the court pointed out, "resulting in poorer chances for higher education." This created a "vicious cycle" where poor districts without accreditation could not recruit new industry and related business to the area. Without new industry, the property and sales tax base will continue to decline, further reducing funds available for schools, the court noted. Differences in spending among poor and wealthy districts in Tennessee varied considerably. Wealthy districts had two times more than poor districts. The court found "a direct correlation between dollars expended and the quality of education a student re-ceives" (*Tennessee Small Sch. Sys. v. McWherter* 1993).

Likewise, the *McDuffy* court in Massachusetts cited evidence that indicated "less affluent school districts were offered significantly fewer educational oppor-tunities and lower educational quality than students in schools in districts where per pupil spending was among the highest of all Commonwealth districts." These high-spending districts, the court said, "are able to educate their children," calling for the state to fulfill its obligation "to educate all its children" (*McDuffy v. Secre-tary of the Executive Office of Education* 1993). The Supreme Judicial Court re-viewed the facts in the case and concluded that the commonwealth was in violation of its constitutional duty to provide all public school students with an "adequate" education. Four of the sixteen towns and cities in which plaintiffs lived and at-tended school (Brockton, Winchendon, Leicester, and Lowell) were compared to wealthier communities with expenditures in the top 25 percent of school spending in the Commonwealth (Brookline, Concord, and Wellesley). The comparisons showed disadvantages for the poorer schools. Inadequacies in these districts re-sulted in fewer educational opportunities and lower educational quality.

Poor districts, the high court noted, had inferior educational programs and condi-tions, including crowded classes; reduced staff; inadequate teaching of basic sub-jects, including reading, writing, science, social studies, mathematics, computers, and other areas; neglected libraries; the inability to attract and retain high-quality teachers; lack of teacher training; lack of curriculum development; *lack of predict-able funding;* administrative reductions; and inadequate guidance counseling. In contrast, wealthy districts had multifaceted reading programs, extensive writing programs and resources, thorough computer instruction, active curriculum develop-ment and review ensuring a comprehensive and up-to-date curriculum, extensive teacher training and development, comprehensive and system-wide student services, and a wide variety of courses in the visual and performing arts. Funding levels in plaintiff schools were "substantially less" than in public schools in other towns and cities, rendering poor localities "unable to furnish students an adequate education." Plaintiffs claimed the state funding system was responsible for "wide disparities" and "insufficiencies" in education support, a finding of the Supreme Judicial Court (*McDuffy v. Secretary of the Executive Office of Education* 1993).

In Vermont the high court pointed out that school districts of equal size but unequal funding would not have "the capacity to offer equivalent foreign language training, purchase equivalent computer technology, hire teachers and other professional personnel of equivalent training and experience, or provide equivalent salaries and benefits." Taking aim directly at the property tax as both a revenue source and mainstay of fiscal disparity, the Vermont Supreme Court invalidated the finance system and stated that local fiscal choice for poor districts was "illusory" and that "nowhere [does the constitution state] that the revenue for education must be raised locally, that the source of the revenue must be property taxes" (*Brigham v. State* 1997).

In finding the Ohio finance system unconstitutional the high court said:

> We find that exhaustive evidence was presented to establish that the appellant school districts were starved for funds, lacked teachers, buildings, and equipment, and had inferior educational programs, and that their pupils were being deprived of educational opportunity. (*DeRolph I*)

Testimony cited in the opinion revealed that under the school finance system the amount of money that supported Ohio schools bore no relationship to the actual *cost* of educating a student—a finding in other courts as well, such as those in New Jersey and Wyoming. A substantial part of the opinion addressed the appalling condition of Ohio's school facilities, including accommodations for children with disabilities.

Citing the "dirty, depressing" conditions of the schools young children attended, the Ohio high court also reviewed evidence of unsafe conditions in the schools. For example, in one school district 300 students were hospitalized because carbon monoxide leaked out of heaters and furnaces. Asbestos was present in 68.6 percent of Ohio's school buildings and a scant 30 percent had adequate fire alarm systems and exterior doors. Roofs leaked, outdated sewage systems caused raw sewage to flow onto the baseball field, and certain schools had arsenic in the drinking water. In other schools, cockroaches crawled on the restroom floors and plaster was falling off the walls. Only 20 percent of the buildings had satisfactory handicapped access. The court noted:

Deering Elementary is not handicapped accessible. The library is a former stor-
age area located in the basement. Handicapped students have to be carried there
and to other locations in the building. One handicapped third-grader at Deering
had never been to the school library because it was inaccessible to someone in a
wheelchair. (*DeRolph I*)

At a later date, the Ohio court opined, "It is the constitutional duty of this State's
General Assembly to provide this State's students with the necessary tools to
choose their direction in life" (*DeRolph v. State of Ohio* 1999).

In Arizona, the high court reviewed and found the capital outlay provisions of
the state finance system unconstitutional. According to the facts presented in the
case, facilities varied enormously across the state and were directly proportional to
the value of real property within the district, including commercial property and
power plants. For example, the high court said:

There are disparities in the number of schools, their condition, their age, and the
quality of classrooms and equipment. Some districts have schools that are unsafe, unhealthy and in violation of building, fire and safety codes. Some districts
use dirt lots for playgrounds. There are schools without libraries, science laboratories, computer rooms, art programs, gymnasiums, and auditoriums. But in
other districts, there are schools with indoor swimming pools, a domed stadium,
science laboratories, television studios, well stocked libraries, satellite dishes,
and extensive computer systems. (*Roosevelt Elementary School District No 66
v. Bishop* 1994)

Facility disparities, the court pointed out, resulted from heavy reliance on local
property tax revenues, which also vary enormously across the state. For instance,
the assessed value of Ruth Fisher Elementary School District, with the highest val-
uation per pupil in the state, was $5.8 million. In San Carlos Unified District, the
poorest, it was $749. Moreover, a property-poor district with a high tax rate could
generate less revenue than a property rich district with a low tax rate because a
property poor district had a small tax base.

In Arkansas, finding the finance system inequitable, inadequate, and unconstitutional, the high court recounted Arkansas' "abysmal rankings in certain key
areas respecting education." The court found, for example, that Arkansas ranked
fiftieth among the states in per capita state and local government expenditures
for elementary and secondary education and between forty-ninth and fiftieth
among the states in teacher's pay. In addition, there were serious disparities in
teachers' salaries and "poor districts with the most ill-prepared students [were]
losing their teachers due to low pay" (*Lake View School District No. 25 v.
Huckabee* 2002). Citing a "few examples" of conditions in schools, the high

court noted that in Lake View School District, with 94 percent of the students on free and reduced price lunches

> there is one uncertified mathematics teacher who teaches all high school mathematics courses. He is paid $10,000 a year as a substitute teacher and works a second job as a school bus driver, earning $5,000 a year. He has an insufficient number of calculators, too few electrical outlets, no compasses and one chalkboard, a computer lacking software and a printer that does not work, an inadequate supply of paper, and a duplicating machine that is overworked ... . The college remediation rate for Lake View is 100 percent. (*Lake View v. Huckabee* 2002)

In Arkansas' Holly Grove School District there were no advanced courses, the court noted. The buildings had leaky roofs and restrooms needed repair. The Barton Elementary School had two bathrooms with four stalls for more than 100 students, and Lee County Schools had no advanced placement classes, school buildings need repair, school buses did not meet state standards, and there were only thirty computers for 600 students.

In April 1999, the South Carolina Supreme Court, reinstating the school finance case, declared that all children are entitled to a "minimally adequate" education, establishing a qualitative standard and affirmative duty of the state toward schooling. Defining with "deliberately broad parameters" the outlines of the constitution's requirement, the high court said the state must provide safe and adequate facilities in which students will have the opportunity to acquire (1) the ability to read, write, and speak the English language and knowledge of mathematics and physical science; (2) a fundamental knowledge of economics, social and political systems, and history and governmental processes; and (3) academic and vocational skills (*Abbeville County School District, et al. v. the State of South Carolina* 15–16 of 21).[5] After considering numerous examples of inequities in school environments, including "buildings in shoddy condition; a lack of necessary equipment including books and other basic supplies; a high level of teacher turnover, due to low salaries and benefits; and overcrowding in districts that serve low-income students as well as increasing numbers of English language learners and falling graduation rates," the Supreme Court remanded the case for trial (*Abbeville County School District et al. v. State of South Carolina* 1999).

In North Carolina the high court in *Leandro* held that unequal funding did not violate constitutional principles and addressed adequacy directly when it asked: Does the right to an education have a qualitative content? Is the state required to provide children with an education that meets some minimum standard? The court answered yes. "An education that does not serve the purpose of preparing students to participate and compete in the society in which they live and work is devoid of substance and is constitutionally inadequate." To determine educational adequacy, the court said, several factors should be considered, including educational goals and standards adopted by the legislature, the achievement of children on standard achievement tests, and per-pupil expenditures, but other factors may be relevant and no single factor may be treated as absolutely authoritative (*Leandro v. North Carolina* 1997).

The case was remanded to the lower court to determine if the funding and substance of the state educational system was constitutionally adequate. Subsequently, the Supreme Court of North Carolina in *Hoke County v. State* (2004) held that the opportunity for students to receive a sound basic education had been violated. Test scores, graduation rates, dropout rates, postsecondary education performance, and employment rates comprised the "outputs" indicators of interest to the court. The evidence showed that "Hoke County students are failing to achieve Level III proficiency in numbers far beyond the state average." In grades 3 to 8, Hoke County trailed the state average in each grade, "with gaps ranging from 11.7 percent to 15.1 percent." It had the "worst retention rate in the state's 100 counties." The county's major employers testified that local graduates were "not qualified to perform even basic tasks that are needed for the jobs available" and that a "high school diploma failed to provide graduates with the skills necessary to compete on an equal basis with others in contemporary society's gainful employment ranks." In addition, the court found, "55 percent of Hoke County graduates attending community college in 1996 were placed in one or more remedial classes for core subjects"—and averaged a D+ in the remedial reading classes and a C– in the remedial math. In regular math and science courses at the community college level, the average grades were both D+. At the University of North Carolina, Hoke County students were required to take remedial courses "at nearly double the rate of their statewide counterparts," received lower grades, and graduated at lower rates. Only one third of the students entering the system graduated five years later (*Hoke County v. State of North Carolina* 2004).

In New York, finding the finance system unconstitutional, the high court in *Campaign for Fiscal Equity v. State* asked whether insufficient funding led to inadequate inputs, which led to unsatisfactory results. The answer was affirmative. As the Court opined, "considering all of the inputs, we conclude ... New York City schools are inadequate ... . Tens of thousands of students are placed in overcrowded classrooms, taught by unqualified teachers, and provided with inadequate facilities and equipment. The number of children in these straits is large enough to represent a systemic failure" (*Campaign for Fiscal Equity v. State* 2003).

The New York Court reviewed resource inputs and outputs, including teaching, facilities, and instrumentalities of learning. The most important input is teaching, the court found, reviewing certification rates, test results, experience levels, and the ratings teachers received from their principals. There was a "mismatch between needs in New York City and the quality of the teaching directed to that need ... . Uncertified or inexperienced teachers tend to be concentrated in the lowest performing schools ... and the longer students are exposed to good or bad teachers, the better or worse they perform." In New York City, 84 percent of the student population was minority, and most were poor. Of the teaching force, 17 percent were either uncertified or taught in areas outside their certification, and the largest percentage of teachers with two or fewer years experience (novices) taught in the city. Teachers had high failure rates on the certification exam—for example, above 40 percent in math. Further, the city schools could neither attract nor retain quality teachers and "the quality of the teaching correlates with student performance" (*Campaign for Fiscal Equity v. State* 2003).

In addition, 31 New York City high schools serving more than 16,000 students had no science laboratory, and there was an "encroachment" of ordinary classroom activities on other specialized spaces, such as libraries, laboratories, and auditoriums. Schools had "excessive class sizes." More than half of all city school children were in classes of 26 or more, and "tens of thousands [were] in classes of over 30." Instrumentalities of learning were also deficient. Many library books were "old and not integrated with contemporary curricula" (*Campaign for Fiscal Equity v. State* 2003). City schools had half as many computers as other schools in New York. They were also aging and unable to support software.

Defendants argued, in part, that high dropout rates and low test scores in city schools resulted from students' low socioeconomic status independent of the quality of the schools. However, the high court held that "we cannot accept the premise that children come to New York City schools uneducable, unfit to learn" (*Campaign for Fiscal Equity v. State* 2003). The high court admonished: "As the trial court correctly observed, this opportunity [for a sound basic education] must still 'be placed within reach of all students,' including those who present with socioeconomic deficits."[6]

Williams v. State, settled out of court in 2004, was California's most recent attempt to address issues of adequacy in funding for K–12 education. The original complaint claimed "all too many California school children must go to schools that shock the conscience." The complaint recounted appalling conditions in the schools, such as students attempting to learn "without books and sometimes without any teachers, and in schools that lack functioning heating or air conditioning systems, that lack sufficient numbers of functioning toilets, and that are infested with vermin, including rats, mice, and cockroaches" (*Williams v. State*). These substandard conditions overwhelmingly exist in schools with students that are low-income, non-white, and English language learners.

At California's Balboa High School, "some students have never taken a book home for homework in as many as three years of attending high school," and at San Francisco's Bryant Elementary School, "the air conditioning and heat do not work in many classrooms ... . Teachers have to spray students with water to keep them cool during spring, summer, and fall." Students at Mark Keppel High School in Alhambra had economics texts that were "last updated in 1986," while "an advanced placement text used at the school was last updated in the 1960s." In addition to this lack of basic resources, temperatures "reached as high as 120 degrees in a class taught in a corrugated metal shed." Thomas Jefferson High School had only "one college counselor to serve the entire school of approximately 3500 students" (*Williams v. State*). An out-of-court settlement reached in August 2004 included provision for school repairs, instructional materials, and the creation of facilities and resource plans.

Two high court opinions filed in Kansas in 2005 responded to plaintiff arguments that the Kansas School District Finance and Quality Performance Act increased discrepancies in revenues available to students, especially those in middle-sized and large districts with a high proportion of minority, at-risk, and special education students.[7] The court overturned the system, finding the legislature had failed to meet its constitutional obligation to provide for a "suitable education." Later, again finding the system unconstitutional, the court held that the constitutional infirmities of the funding system had not been remedied by legislative action (*Montoy v. State of Kansas* 2005). Inequalities among Kansas school districts were tremendous—in excess of 300 percent between the highest and lowest spending districts. For example, the court noted, in "U.S.D. 480 (Liberal), funding is $5,655.95, while students in U.S.D. 301 (Nes Tres La Go) receive the highest per pupil FTE allotment of $16,968.49" (*Montoy v. State* 2003). Funding inequalities resulted in performance inequalities. According to the court, "Many Kansas teachers, in large classes, only have time to 'teach to the middle,' that is they must tailor their presentations to the perhaps fictitious 'average' student with no time or resources to really help those at either end of the achievement spectrum." Moreover, the court said, when student performance data are disaggregated, "it becomes clear that many categories of Kansas students (minorities, the poor, children with disabilities, and English language learners) are failing at alarming rates" (*Montoy v. State* 2005). The data showed that

> 83.7 percent of Kansas African American students, 81.1 percent of Kansas Hispanic students, 64.1 percent of Kansas Native American students, 79.8 percent of Kansas disabled students, 87.1 percent of Kansas limited English proficiency students, and 77.5 percent of Kansas impoverished students are failing 10th grade math. (*Montoy v. State* 2005)

School failure data underestimate the problem because dropout rates among these populations are also increasing. The superintendent of Wichita public schools described the achievement gap as "stunning." The State Commissioner of Education said the state-wide achievement gap "would take your breath away." The court held that this information "conclusively demonstrates the adverse and unconstitutional disparate impact the current funding scheme has on our most vulnerable and/or protected students" (*Montoy v. State* 2005).

Summary and Discussion

The analysis of judicial decisions emerging during the new wave of school finance litigation shows that schools in America are rich, they are poor, they are unequal and inadequate. Evidence presented in these cases illustrates savage inequalities and inadequacies that plague America's schools, providing the least resources
to those who need them most: low- income students, students of color, and other
students with special educational needs.

The California complaint cited schools that "shock the conscience." In Alaska it
is alleged that "Every Alaskan child receives an inadequate education because the
funding of that education is grossly inadequate." Kentucky experts testified that
"without exception, there is great disparity among poor and wealthy districts in
Kentucky regarding basic educational materials; student-teacher ratio; curriculum;
size, adequacy and condition of physical plant; and quality of basic management."
In Montana comparisons of similarly sized high- and low-spending school districts
showed advantages for high-spending districts such as "greater budget flexibility
to address educational needs and goals," enriched and expanded curricula, and
better equipped and better facilities. The *Edgewood* decision in Texas highlighted
gross disparities among school districts. San Elizario Independent School District
offered no foreign language, no prekindergarten program, no chemistry, no physics, no calculus, and no college preparatory or honors program. Extracurricular
programs were almost nonexistent. There was no band, debate, or football. On the
other hand, high wealth districts were able to provide for their students' broader
educational experiences, including more extensive curricula, lower student-teacher ratios, better facilities, parental involvement programs, and dropout prevention
programs.

In New Jersey (*Abbott II*) the court noted that the poorer the district, the greater its
need, the less the money available, and the worse the education. Likewise, the Tennessee high court said lack of funds prevented poor schools from offering advanced
placement courses, more than one foreign language at a high school, state-mandated
art and music classes, drama instruction, and extracurricular athletic teams.

In Massachusetts the *McDuffy* court cited evidence that indicated "less affluent
school districts were offered significantly fewer educational opportunities and
lower educational quality than students in schools in districts where per pupil
spending was among the highest of all Commonwealth districts." The Vermont
court opined that school districts of equal size but unequal funding would not have
"the capacity to offer equivalent foreign language training, purchase equivalent
computer technology, hire teachers and other professional personnel of equivalent
training and experience, or provide equivalent salaries and benefits." In Ohio the
high court cited the "dirty, depressing" conditions of the schools young children attended and the unsafe conditions that existed in the schools. For example, asbestos
was present in 68.6 percent of Ohio's school buildings and a scant 30 percent had

adequate fire alarm systems and exterior doors. There were leaking roofs, outdated sewage systems that caused raw sewage to flow onto the baseball field, and arsenic in the drinking water of certain schools. In other schools, cockroaches crawled on the restroom floors and plaster was falling off of the walls. Only 20 percent of the buildings had satisfactory handicapped access.

In Arizona the high court found disparities in the number of schools, their condition, their age, and the quality of classrooms and equipment. Some districts have schools that are unsafe, unhealthy, and in violation of building, fire, and safety codes. The Arkansas court noted serious disparities in teachers' salaries and that "poor districts with the most ill-prepared students are losing their teachers due to low pay." In New York the high court held that "tens of thousands of students are placed in overcrowded classrooms, taught by unqualified teachers, and provided with inadequate facilities and equipment." California's complaint recounted students attempting to learn "without books and sometimes without any teachers, and in schools that lack functioning heating or air conditioning systems, that lack sufficient numbers of functioning toilets, and that are infested with vermin, including rats, mice, and cockroaches."

In these rulings and others like them, state high courts are invoking a substantive, "qualitative" standard that defines the contours of an adequate education to which all children are entitled and which will equip them to be citizens and competitors in the knowledge society and global economy. The courts have concluded that savage inequalities and gross inadequacy in state education systems erect substantial barriers to the realization of equal opportunities for quality education across the states and the nation. Is it fair that some children, through no fault of their own—like Skye in Aniak Elementary School in Alaska—begin school with the deck stacked against them? Where success can only be found in spite of the appalling and inadequate public education system to which they are consigned? In response to questions like this, the Ohio court quoted from Robert Frost:

The Road Not Taken

Two roads diverged in a yellow wood,
And sorry I could not travel both
And be one traveler, long I stood
And looked down one as far as I could
To where it bent in the undergrowth;
Then took the other, as just as fair,
And having perhaps the better claim,
Because it was grassy and wanted wear;
Though as far that the passing there
Had worn them really about the same,
And both that morning equally lay

In leaves no step had trodden black.
Oh, I kept the first for another day!
Yet knowing how way leads on to way,
I doubted if I should ever come back.
I shall be telling this with a sigh
Somewhere ages and ages hence;
Two roads diverged in a wood, and I—
I took the one less traveled by,
And that has made all the difference.

According to the court, "All the children of this State are entitled to the opportunity to better themselves and to choose their lot in life ... to choose their own path and not be faced with roadblocks to their future which a lack of school funding creates" (*DeRolph v. State of Ohio* 1999).

America prides itself on justice and liberty for all, yet the shame of America's schools for children of color, the poor and others fundamentally challenges this notion. The inequalities documented by Jonathan Kozol's *Savage Inequalities* have not lessened over the past decade and a half. In fact, today we witness entire states in which school funding is found to be inadequate, unsatisfactory, and insufficient, creating an affront to any standard of decency and caring for America's future—its children and youth.

Notes

1. This excerpt draws heavily on *Kristine Moore v. State of Alaska,* First Amended Complaint, Dec. 3, 2003 (Case No. 3AN-04-9756 Civ.).
2. The Kentucky Supreme Court accepted the trial court's statement that an "efficient" educational system, as required by the constitution, was uniform, unitary, and adequate. An adequate system must provide each child with facility in seven essential competencies, the court said. These include

- Sufficient oral and written communication skills to enable students to function in a complex and rapidly changing civilization
- Sufficient knowledge of economic, social, and political systems to enable the student to make informed choices
- Sufficient understanding of governmental processes to enable the student to understand the issues that affect his or her community, state, and nation
- Sufficient self-knowledge and knowledge of his or her mental and physical wellness
- Sufficient grounding in the arts to enable each student to appreciate his or her cultural and historical heritage
- Sufficient training or preparation for advanced training in either academic or vocational fields so as to enable each child to choose and pursue life work intelligently
- Sufficient levels of academic or vocational skills to enable public school students to compete favorably with their counterparts in surrounding states, in academics or in the job market

The lower courts in Ohio and Alabama and the high court in Massachusetts, New Hampshire, and Arkansas also found that an adequate education system sought to ensure each student the "seven essential competencies" cited in Kentucky, including a *"sufficient level of academic or vocational skills to enable him or her to compete favorably with counterparts in surrounding states. "* To this the Alabama court added that each student should be able to compete favorably not only among surrounding states but also "across the nation, and throughout the world, in academics or the job market."

3. See *Abbott v. Burke,* 495 A.2d, 381; *Abbott v. Burke (Abbott II),* 575 A.2d 359, 363; *Abbott v. Burke (Abbott III),* 643 A.2d 575, 576; *Abbott v. Burke (Abbott IV),* 693 A.2d 417, 420–32; *Abbott v. Burke (Abbott V),* 710 A.2d 450, 454; *Abbott v. Burke (Abbott VI),* 748 A.2d 85; and *Abbott v. Burke (Abbott VII),* 790 A.2d 842, 845.
Brigham v. State, 692 A.2d 384 (Vermont, 1997), 390.

4. In *Abbott V* the court substantially accepted the State's plan for improving urban schools. See also *Abbott VII* in which the New Jersey Supreme Court in May 2000 finds that the state must fully fund all facilities improvements and new construction in Abbott districts. *Abbott v. Burke* 751 A.2d 1032. For a fuller discussion, see Goertz (2001).

5. See also, Fogle (2000).

6. The high court here is commenting on immigrants and declines "to pin the blame" solely on the deficits a "troubled child" brings with him to schools. There is no proof that dropout rates result from high numbers of teenage immigrants who enter ninth grade unable to graduate. Instead, poor completion rates of high school students in New York City schools result from learning deficits that begin to be accumulated long before high school (*Campaign for Fiscal Equity v. State of New York*).

7. See *Montoy v. State of Kansas* 112 P.3d 1160 (Kansas, 2005), opinion filed January 3, 2005 in which the court reversed the district court's holding that the financing formula in School District Finance and Quality Performance Act (SDFQPA) was a violation of equal protection and that the SDFQPA financing formula had an unconstitutional disparate impact on minorities and other classes. The court affirmed the district court holding that the legislature failed to meet its constitutional obligation to provide for a suitable education. In the second opinion, *Montoy v. State of Kansas* 112 P.3d 923 (Kansas, 2005), the court found that House Bill 2247 failed to remedy the constitutional infirmities of SDFQPA.

References

Abbeville County School District, et al. v. the State of South Carolina, 515 S.E.2d 535 (S.C. 1999).
Abbott v. Burke, 495 A.2d, 381 (N.J. 1985).
Abbott v. Burke (Abbott II), 575 A.2d at 375, 383, 395–397, 400–401 (N.J. 1990).
Abbott v. Burke (Abbott III), 643 A.2d 575, 576 (N.J. 1994).
Abbott v. Burke (Abbott IV), 693 A.2d 417, 420–32 (N.J. 1997).
Abbott v. Burke (Abbott V), 710 A.2d 450, 454 (N.J. 1998).
Abbott v. Burke (Abbott VI), 748 A.2d 82, 85 (N.J. 2000).
Abbott v. Burke (Abbott VII), 790 A.2d 842, 845 (N.J. 2002).
Brigham v. State, 692 A.2d 384 (Vt. 1997), 390.
Campaign for Fiscal Equity, Inc. v. State, 801 N.E.2d 326, 336 (N.Y. 2003).
DeRolph I, 677 N.E.2d 733 at 742 (Ohio 1997).
DeRolph et al. v. The State of Ohio et al., 712 N.E.2d 125 at 254 (Ohio 1999).
Fogle, Jennifer L. 2000. *Abbeville County School District v. State: The Right of a Minimally Adequate Education in South Carolina.* 51 S.C.L. Rev. 420.
Goertz, Margaret. 2001. "New Jersey School Finance in the New Millenium." In *School Finance Litigation Across the States: An Update.* (EA 031155/ED 455595). Edited by Deborah A. Verstegen. ERIC Clearinghouse on Educational Management, College of Education-University of Oregon.

Helena Elementary School District v. State, 769 O, 2d 684m 689–90 (Mont. 1989). Opinion amended by 784 P.2d 412 (Mont. 1990).

Hoke County Board of Education et al. v. State of North Carolina, 599 S.E.2d 365, at 383 (N.C. 2004).

Kozol, Jonathan. 1991. *Savage Inequalities: Children in America@146>s Schools.* New York: Crown.

Kristine Moore v. State of Alaska, First Amended Complaint for Declaratory and Injunctive Relief, Case No. 3AN-04-9756 Civ.

Lake View School District No. 25 v. Huckabee, 91 S.W.3d 472, 488 (Ark. 2002).

Leandro v. North Carolina, 488 S.E. 2d 249, 254, 256 (N.C. 1997).

McDuffy v. Secretary of the Executive Office of Education, 615 N.E.2d 516 (Mass. 1993), 521.

Montoy v. State of Kansas, No. 99-C-1738, memorandum decision and preliminary interim order (Kan. Dec. 2, 2003). http://www.shawneecourt.org/decisions/99c1738a2.htm

Montoy v. State of Kansas, 112 P.3d 1160 (Kan. 2005).

Roosevelt Elementary School District No 66 v. Bishop, 877 P.2d 806, 808 (Ariz. 1994).

Rose v. Council for Better Education, Inc., 790 S.W.2d 186 (Ky. 1989).

Tennessee Small School System v.McWherter, 851 S.W.2d 139 (Tenn. 1993), 144.

Verstegen, Deborah A. 1994. "The New Wave of School Finance Litigation." *Phi Delta Kappan* 76:243–250.

———. 2002. "Financing Adequacy: Towards New Models of Education Finance That Support Standards-Based Reform." *Journal of Education Finance* 27:749–781.

———. 2004a. "Calculation of the Cost of and Adequate Education in Kentucky Using the Professional Judgement Approach." *Education Policy Analysis Archives* 12:1–36. http://epaa.asu.edu/apaa/v12n8/

———. 2004b. "Towards a Theory of Adequacy: The Continuing Saga of Equal Educational Opportunity in the Context of State Constitutional Challenges to School Finance Systems." *Saint Louis University Public Law Review* 33:499–530.

Williams v. California, Superior Court of the State of California County of San Francisco, No. 312236, First Amended Complaint for Injunctive and Declaratory Relief.

Correspondence should be addressed to Deborah Verstegen, Professor and Chair, Department of Educational Leadership, University of Nevada, MS 283, College of Education, 4054, Reno, NV. E-mail: dav3e@unr.edu

BOOK REVIEWS

The Shame of the Nation: The Restoration of Apartheid Schooling in America. Jonathan Kozol. New York: Crown, 2005. 404 pp. $25 (hard cover).

AMY STUART WELLS
Teachers College, Columbia University

Jonathan Kozol has never been one to mince words or sugar-coat his message about how profoundly unfair life is for poor blacks and Hispanics in this country. For the last three and a half decades, Kozol has written books about poor people of color and the layers of injustice they face in public schools and our society in general. In all these years, he has never lost his ability to tell it like it is—to lay bare the grand American contradiction between our ideals of equality and our highly unequal society.

Yet what is most amazing about Kozol's books is not that he writes them but that so many people, inside and outside of academia, read and cite them. His popularity suggests that thousands, even millions, of Americans concur with him that the most affluent country on the globe should not allow so many of its children to live in abject poverty and attend falling-down schools with poorly trained teachers and nonfunctioning toilets. Still, so much of what Kozol writes about has not changed, and in some cases has gotten worse, since he began chronicling poor kids' lives in the late 1960s. It must be, therefore, that the vast majority of his readers are baffled by the enormity of the problem and the lack of politically convenient solutions—or are we just too vested in the status quo? We read his books, weep, and then go about our lives.

The political movements necessary to change the conditions Kozol writes about have not materialized. In fact, the only tangible school reform effort that has been re-energized in part because of Kozol's writings is school finance litigation. Indeed, the noble lawyers who fight for more money for poor schools and students have clearly been galvanized by his work. References to Kozol's 1991 book, *Savage Inequalities*, are found throughout the legal and social science literature on school finance.

This is more than a little ironic given that Kozol's latest book, *The Shame of the Nation: The Restoration of Apartheid Schooling in America* (2005), is a 300-page argument about why changes neither in school funding nor in the popular high-stakes accountability policies will solve the problem of apartheid schooling and the inequality it perpetuates. In this new book, Kozol steps out onto a far more fragile limb than even he has dared to traipse upon in the past. In some ways he is covering old ground; in other ways, he is ratcheting the discussion of inequality up a notch, challenging comfortable suburbanites and affluent urbanites in a more direct way that is likely to make us all uncomfortable.

The Same Kozol, Only Different: Why Segregation Matters Most

The Shame of the Nation is, on one hand, familiarly Kozol. It is another vivid reminder of the yawning gap between our rhetoric and our reality. It is, like Kozol books past, unapologetically straightforward and straight shooting. Indeed, in this new installment of the Kozol canon on U.S. hypocrisy he quotes Thomas Merton, who wrote that we are obliged, at certain times, "to say what things are and to give them their right names" (10).

Clearly, this is, and has been, Kozol's mantra, and those of us who come along for the ride should be prepared to be outraged and, in the end, highly frustrated and annoyed. And yet, the distance between the problem and the possibility of meaningful change is even more profound in *The Shame of the Nation* than it was in prior Kozol books such as the best-selling *Savage Inequalities* (1991) or *Amazing Grace* (1995)—or even his first book, *Death at an Early Age* (1967). These earlier books, as disturbing as they were in their portrayals of poor children and their schools and communities, did not get to the heart of the matter of how this inequality is maintained, justified, and even legitimized. The subject of apartheid, or extreme and persistent degrees of racial segregation in the United States, is *the* unifying theme of this latest book, as its subtitle suggests. The argument Kozol makes here is the same one the Supreme Court made in its landmark *Brown v. Board of Education* decision in 1954: "separate is inherently unequal."

While Kozol certainly acknowledged racial segregation in his prior writing, it was in the background of these other books as he remained more focused on the children, the adults who surrounded them, and the deplorable condition of their schools and neighborhoods. In *The Shame of the Nation*, segregation itself is front and center, and while Kozol notes that it may not be the only cause of poverty and inequality, he argues that it is the best explanation of why such depravation is allowed to continue to exist within an affluent society.

Kozol's point—threaded through descriptions of mind-numbing reading lessons and overcrowded lunch hours in really poor, all-black and Latino schools—is that if these children went to school with more affluent, white or Asian classmates, they would not be subject to the same kind of inhumane conditions and treatment. It's as if Kozol is inviting us to imagine a society in which all the schools are racially balanced and all the poor children are evenly dispersed into predominantly middle-class schools. Would any of these schools, Kozol wants to know, have the kind of pervasive "prepackaged," dumbed-down, automated, and stifling curriculum and teaching found in so many impoverished schools today? Would any of them have grossly underprepared teachers who talk about whole schools of students as if they were robots training for the lowest level jobs? Would elected officials allow these pretend schools, serving the offspring of more politically powerful parents, to be as overcrowded and decrepit as the schools in East Los Angeles, the South Bronx, or Roosevelt, Long Island?

The answer is "no" to all of the above, and yet, we refuse, as a nation, to wrap our heads around the relationship between racial segregation and inequality. It is that very relationship that the U.S. Supreme Court addressed in the 1954 *Brown* decision:

> We come then to the question presented: Does segregation of children in public schools solely on the basis of race, even though the physical facilities and other "tangible" factors may be equal, deprive the children of the minority group of equal educational opportunities? We believe that it does.

In other words, the Supreme Court argued, even if we could somehow assure that segregated black and white schools had the exact same number of books, microscopes, pencils, or other tangible factors, the mere fact that they were separate schools based upon the race of the students would make them unequal. The Court provided two intertwined explanations for its conclusion. First of all, citing several prior cases involving African Americans' access to segregated white universities, the court noted the importance of "intangible" factors associated with schools—be they law schools, graduate schools, or elementary and secondary schools. Such intangible factors include the qualities of a school that are "incapable of objective measurement," but which make for "greatness" (or at least the perception of it)—for example, its reputation, the esteem of its faculty, and the professional networks and connections of faculty and students, all of which benefit students long after graduation.

Second, the Supreme Court noted that such considerations apply "with added force" to children in grade school and high school because of the social psychological research Kenneth and Mamie Clark presented as part of the *Brown* case. The Clarks' work demonstrated the sense of racial inferiority that very young black children developed within racially segregated contexts. In perhaps the most famous quote of this landmark decision, the Court stated: "To separate them [black students] from others of similar age and qualifications solely because of their race generates a feeling of inferiority as to their status in the community that may affect their hearts and minds in a way unlikely ever to be undone" (5).

School desegregation, therefore, was never about black children needing to sit next to white children to learn—an assumption made and then scoffed upon by many of its detractors. Rather, it was about having a seat at the table in schools deemed to be the "best" and most highly valued in this society—the schools that, because of their prestige and reputation, open doors for their graduates in ways poorer schools cannot. Along with institutional prestige comes a set of expectations and a culture of academic privilege that attracts some of the best prepared teachers and translates into a challenging curriculum and a high success rate for graduates. In this way, the intangible becomes tangible, and the cost of depriving someone of access to the "better" schools because of race becomes quite high. Whether that deprivation is codified in a *de jure* law of strict racial separation or maintained via slightly more subtle forms of racial exclusion, such as housing and job discrimination, matters little for the poor black or Latino child who lacks access to the most prestigious schools. These students are forced to digest the understanding that they have been repeatedly denied what is good enough for white, middle-class children (Crain et al. 1992).

And then, of course, there is the "Can we all get along?" factor—the idea that by going to school with students of different racial/ethnic backgrounds children will learn how to be with people who are not like them. Kozol speaks to the importance of children learning to know each other across racial and socioeconomic barriers, and a growing body of social science research supports that argument. In fact, we know that *all* children are better prepared for a racially diverse society if they attend integrated schools. For instance, in a recent study my colleagues and I conducted we found that nearly 250 whites, blacks, and Latinos who graduated from desegregated high schools in 1980 said that, even as adults, they find their integration experience valuable because it allowed them to cross rigid racial boundaries that defined their lives outside of school. They all noted that more than twenty years later they remain much more comfortable in racially diverse settings than their spouses, parents, or friends who attended segregated schools (see Wells et al. 2004). These findings jibe with those of an extensive literature review on the long-term impact of school desegregation on the lives of African Americans (Wells and Crain 1994). Overall, this literature reveals that blacks who attend more racially diverse schools are more likely to attend predominantly white colleges and universities and are more likely to hold jobs in mostly white firms and industries and live in integrated neighborhoods than are blacks who went to all-black schools.

Similarly, social science research entered into evidence in the Supreme Court case regarding affirmative action for law schools, *Grutter v. Bollinger,* concluded that university students who attended more diverse schools showed significantly greater motivation to take the perspective of others and expressed a greater sense of commonality in values about work and family with groups other than their own (Gurin 2005). Another finding was that university students "learn more and think in deeper, more complex ways in a diverse educational environment" (Gurin 2005, 1). Thus, reams of research and our common sense tells us that people of different racial backgrounds who go to school together are better able to get along as adults and that diversity makes them think about issues in a more complicated way.

But what about the infamous black-white test score gap that so many policy makers are bent on closing? Can we hope to close this gap via policies that hold educators accountable for helping all children achieve to high levels in racially segregated schools? Can the mandate of the 1896 Supreme Court ruling in *Plessy v. Ferguson* of "separate but equal" ever be realized in a society in which whites hold such a disproportionate amount of power and wealth? These are questions that go to the heart of Kozol's argument in *Shame*. He comes down on the side of integration over segregated accountability—even when segregated urban schools have acquired extra resources via school funding cases. He notes that the black-white test score gap closed more during the peak years of school desegregation than any other time in the history of this country. In fact, since federal judges and local school officials across the country began dismantling desegregation programs in the late 1980s and the number of students attending racially segregated schools has grown, the gap in test scores between blacks and whites has widened. Kozol quotes an African American educator who noted: "Segregated schools will not be equal to the schools attended by the middle class." He argued that no matter what inducements to segregation are made to placate people in the black community, "kids of color will get less and less. History teaches us this if we are willing to learn anything from history" (220).

Furthermore, as Kozol and others point out, the United States has become increasingly diverse as a society, even as our schools have become more racially segregated (Metropolitan Center for Urban Education 2005). Indeed, our public school population is now only 58 percent white, down from 78 percent in 1972. Hispanic students represent 19 percent of public school enrollment, up from 6 percent in 1972, and black students constitute about 17 percent of all public school students.

Meanwhile, white students are less likely to attend school with black and Latino students today than they were 20 years ago, and levels of segregation have been steadily increasing since the 1980s (Orfield and Lee 2005). In fact, between 1991 and 2002, the percentage of African American students attending predominantly black schools grew as much as 10 percent in some areas of the country, and the percentage of Latino students attending predominantly Latino schools grew by as much as 18 percent in some states. In 2002–2003, the average white student attended a school that was almost 80 percent white, while the average black and Latino students attended schools that were 30 percent or less white (Orfield and Lee 2005).

Hand in hand with this growing racial/ethnic segregation is an increased concentration of poverty in predominantly black and/or Latino schools. As Orfield and Lee (2005) report, 88 percent of high minority schools—those more than 90 percent minority—are also high poverty schools, meaning more than 50 percent of the students are on free and reduced lunch. The corresponding share of schools with less than 10 percent minority students that are also high poverty schools is only 15 percent. The correlation between attending a school with a high concentration of poverty and low student achievement is stronger, tighter, and more consistent than probably any other two variables in the field of education.

Kozol reminds us, therefore, that there is ample evidence that racial and social class segregation and isolation are bad for our increasingly diverse country. And yet, at various commemorations of the fiftieth anniversary of *Brown v. Board of Education* in 2004, white speakers in particular tried to gloss over the enormous contradiction of an increasingly diverse and yet increasingly segregated society. Instead, many embraced policies such as the Bush Administration's No Child Left Behind education program, arguing that schools are now being forced via high-stakes accountability mandates to educate *all* students to the same high standards no matter how separate and unequal their schools may be.

Kozol spent many days in some of the poorest and most racially isolated black and Latino schools in order to report just what "high-stakes accountability" looks like from that standpoint. He argues that if the No Child Left Behind Act (NCLB) and the testing regime it has unfurled is our best solution to what ails segregated, low-income schools, we—or rather the children in those schools—are in trouble. Chapter 3 of *Shame*, titled "The Ordering Regime," documents what Kozol calls "an architecture of adaptive strategies" to produce the incremental gains on student standardized test scores within the limits inequality allows. He describes the scripted lessons, the administrative memos, the classroom posters, the "silent" lunches and recesses, and the military salutes—all designed to help the mostly in-experienced and undertrained teachers to raise the test scores of poor children by some incremental amount. Affluent parents, Kozol reminds us, would not stand for a school organized around this highly structured, no-frills, no-laughter, no-fun cur-riculum—what one teacher in a South Bronx school called "primitive utilitarian-ism." His descriptions leave us wondering how NCLB and the phalanx of testing and accountability requirements it established can lead to a racially separate equal-ity when it is mostly poor children of color who are punished by these policies and subjected to pedagogy focused solely on producing higher scores. Kozol suggests that NCLB is yet another scheme for preparing poor children for unimaginative work at the bottom of the service economy.

And then there is the school finance reform movement, that "other" solution to segregation—the one more frequently supported by folks on the political left and certainly by readers of Kozol's earlier books. This solution centers on ensuring that poor schools' levels of state funding are equal to or higher than schools in wealthy communities. Here is where Kozol steps further out onto his limb, arguing that these legal battles over school funding, as well intentioned as they may be, are not only insufficient but can be counterproductive to the more meaningful goal of ra-cial integration. Kozol writes that these school finance cases remind us of how far

the nation has retreated from the high ideals and purposes identified in the Supreme Court's *Brown* ruling. He notes that lawyers for the plaintiffs in poor and
underfunded school districts, which are almost always majority black and/or Latino, rarely choose to speak at all of racial isolation:

> Indeed, the argument in almost all these cases rests implicitly upon the premise
> that the ... [Supreme] Court was incorrect in its decision and that separate edu-
> cation can be rendered, if not equal, at least good enough to be sufficient for the
> children who attend school in a segregated system. If attorneys were to argue
> that the finding in *Brown v. Board of Education* was correct, it would be difficult
> to make the case that funding increments will bring sufficient gains to segre-
> gated children to be worth the court's consideration. (259)

Indeed, Kozol finds it somewhat ironic that lawyers representing poor students
in these so-called adequacy school finance cases often make allusions to *Brown*
while seemingly ignoring the Warren Court's insistence on the damage done to
children by their racial segregation and the argument that in the field of education,
the doctrine of "separate but equal" has no place. "Yet," Kozol notes, "separate but
equal obviously has to have a place within these equity or adequacy cases" (260).

It May Be the Right Thing to Do, But That Doesn't Mean We Will Do It

After all is said and done, attacking apartheid is fundamentally different than
calling for more funding for poor children. Solving racial segregation in public education would require far more than shifting some money from suburban tax payers to urban schools. It would require residents of affluent suburbs to open their
communities, schools, and classrooms to the children they left behind when they
moved to these predominantly white, Asian, and affluent enclaves. Whether they
admit it or not, their point in moving to suburbia or enrolling their children in elite
private schools was to get away from poor people. And while most white folks
would deny that they fled cities and city schools to get away from African American and/or Latino families, it is no coincidence that most poor urban folk in this
country are black or brown.

Resistance to efforts to bring some of those same poor black and brown folk to
the affluent suburban communities and elite schools is likely to be fierce. A case in
point is the Long Island suburb of East Meadow that Kozol writes about. Kozol describes the dire straits of the all black and Latino and mostly poor Roosevelt school
district, which neighbors several predominantly white and affluent communities
such as East Meadow. He then tells the tale of the New York state commissioner
of education's ill-fated proposal to dissolve the impoverished and dysfunctional
Roosevelt district and send its students to surrounding districts, including East

Meadow. Quoting a *New York Times* article, Kozol writes that "the reaction to this proposal on the part of the surrounding districts, said Richard Mills, the commissioner of education ... was 'sheer terror'" (157). In fact, flyers were circulated reading, "KEEP ROOSEVELT STUDENTS OUT OF EAST MEADOW." The smaller print on the flyers made an unconvincing effort, according to Kozol, to insist that this was not a racial issue; it was all about social class. But the flyer described the children as "the low-achieving, dysfunctional, criminal bunch from Roosevelt which the state wants to dump on us" (158). Such language, Kozol reminds us, is not unlike the words that inflamed the fears of white communities throughout the South a generation ago. Similar language, the East Meadow school superintendent told Kozol, was displayed on bumper stickers. The state officials' proposal to dissolve the Roosevelt School District was withdrawn.

The East Meadow story is all too reminiscent of other suburban communities that fought tooth and nail to keep students of color, even very small numbers of them, out of their schools. In affluent Tenafly, New Jersey, residents tied orange ribbons around trees in protest of proposals to allow some black and Latino students from nearby Englewood to transfer to the high school. Meanwhile, white students from near by Englewood Cliffs had been transferring into Tenafly for years (see Wells et al. in press.).

How "liberal" are the residents of places like East Meadow and Tenafly? Perhaps most of them oppose the death penalty and support abortion rights. They may well argue that multiculturalism is a good idea, at least in the abstract, and write checks to the American Red Cross to help the victims of natural disasters. And still, they protest like 1950s Southerners when the mere idea of racial integration of their local schools is floated. Kozol writes:

> White educated people who believe in racial integration as an ultimate ideal, but long ago abandoned public schools in which they had a chance to make it real, will have their old recordings of the songs of freedom that they used to sing when they were young and they may dig them out and play them now and then when they're nostalgic for the days when everything seemed possible ... (274)

Reading *The Shame of the Nation* makes all of us long for those days when *something* seemed possible, but we have seen far more stagnation and regression than progress in racial integration and equality over the last twenty-five years. And yet, most Americans, at some basic level, acknowledge the wisdom of integration as we watch our nation become more racially diverse every year. Opinion polls show that only 16 percent of white parents and 10 percent of black parents say that racial integration is "not important at all" in choosing their own children's schools (Public Agenda 1998). Furthermore, a 2003 telephone survey of 3,421 adults found that a strong majority—57 percent—believed that going to an integrated school was better for their children, and 33 percent believed that it made no difference (Metropolitan Center 2005). With the percentage of white students in our nation's public schools now less than 60 percent, white parents have to wonder whether overwhelmingly white schools can prepare their children for our global society.

Still, it is all too clear that little will change absent a powerful political movement that would, if successful, require affluent people, conservative and liberal, not only to repeal their tax cuts but also to open up their neighborhoods and schools to those they ran away from (literally and figuratively). This seems improbable in the current political context when not a single policy maker or public figure is playing a leadership role on these issues. In a quintessential Kozol testimonial, he writes:

> Certainly, what reasonable people may regard as possible, or even worth consideration in the present political climate of the nation, needs to be addressed; but what is obvious and plain and truthful needs to be addressed as well. If we have agreed to live with this reality essentially unaltered for another generation or for several generations yet to come, I think we need at least to have the honesty to say so. I also think we need to recognize that our acceptance of a dual education system will have consequences that may be no less destructive than those we have seen in the past century ... (11)

If I were to fault Kozol as the author of such a bold and politically out-of-step book, I would say that he could have said more about the few and scattered diverse communities across the country and their struggles to maintain racial balance. He also could have documented racially diverse public schools that manage to survive and occasionally embrace their diversity in a political context that provides them little or no moral or political support. Kozol is also silent on policy proposals that could, if enacted, allow more people to choose racially integrated schools and communities. For instance, we could amend state policies, such as charter school or open enrollment laws, to provide incentives and resources—for example, transportation and outreach—to educators or parents who want to start racially diverse schools of choice. At the same time, the federal and state governments could be doing far more to encourage local officials to adopt zoning regulations that promote mixed-income housing (see Wells et al. 2004).

These are not earth-shattering proposals, and they will not bring about widespread change, but they are better than doing nothing. They could help create the kind of cross-racial interaction and trust that Kozol says we are so lacking as an apartheid nation. Such relatively small-scale proposals—the kind that would be attractive to those willing to take chances—may be our only hope at this moment. They may be the best way to get even small number of whites to put their money where their mouths are, based on the opinion poll data cited previously. They are, at least, a beginning, which is more than we have now.

At the end of *Amazing Grace*, Mrs. Washington, Kozol's friend and informant from the South Bronx, reflects on white people and their views on poor blacks and Latinos. She says, "I think they wish that we were never born" (246). But she adds that she is not talking about *all* whites: "Some are nice people but they can't get nothing done and so they put it out of mind" (246). In some ways, *Shame* reads like Kozol's last bold attempt to put "it" back in our minds. However, he is weary, and we cannot count on him to keep nagging us forever or to come up with all the solutions. Those of us who read Kozol and weep must do more than wring our collective hands and shake our collective heads when we finish this newest book. Shame on us if we fail to act.

References

Crain, Robert L., R. L. Miller, J. A. Hawes, & J. R. Peichert. 1992. *Finding Niches: The Effect of School Desegregation on Black Students.* New York: Institute for Urban Education, Teachers College, Columbia University.

Gurin, Patricia. "Expert Report of Patricia Gurin." *Gratz, et al. v. Bollinger, et al.*, No. 97–75321 (E.D. Mich.) *Grutter, et al. v. Bollinger, et al.*, No. 97–75928 (E.D. Mich.). www.umich.edu/~urel/admissions/research/expert/gurintoc.html

Kozol, Jonathan. 1967. *Death at an Early Age: The Destruction of the Hearts and Minds of Negro Children in the Boston Public Schools.* Boston: Houghton Mifflin.

———. 1991. *Savage Inequalities: Children in America's Schools.* New York: HarperCollins.

———. 1995. *Amazing Grace: The Lives of Children and the Conscience of a Nation.* New York: Crown.

Metropolitan Center for Urban Education. 2005. *With All Deliberate Speed: Achievement, Citizenship and Diversity in American Education.* New York: The Steinhardt School of Education, New York University.

Orfield, Gary, and Chungmei Lee. 2005. *Why Segregation Matters: Poverty and Educational Inequality.* http://www.civilrightsproject.harvard.edu/

Public Agenda. 1998. *Time to Move On: African-American and White Parents Set an Agenda for Public School.* New York: Author.

Wells, Amy Stuart, and Robert L. Crain. 1994. "Perpetuation Theory and the Long-Term Effects of School Desegregation." *Review of Educational Research* 64:531–555.

Wells, Amy Stuart, Jennifer Jellison Holme, Anita Tijerina Revilla, and Awo Korantemaa Atanda. 2004. *How Desegregation Changed Us: The Effects of Racially Mixed Schools on Students and Society.* New York: Teachers College, Columbia University.

Wells, Amy Stuart, Jennifer Jellison Holme, Anita Tijerina Revilla, and Awo Korantemaa Atanda. in press. *Both Sides Now: Looking Back on School Desegregation.* Cambridge, Mass.: Harvard University Press.

Final Test: The Battle for Adequacy in America's Schools. Peter Schrag. New York: The New Press, 2003. 308 pp. $25.95 (cloth).

Class and Schools: Using Social, Economic and Educational Reform to Close the Black-White Achievement Gap. Richard Rothstein. Washington, D.C.: Economic Policy Institute, 2004. 203 pp. $17.95 (paper).

MOLLY TOWNES O'BRIEN
University of Wollongong

When a levee broke and the brackish waters of Lake Pontchartrain flooded into the city of New Orleans, American inequality floated into view along with the flood's flotsam and jetsam. One might expect a flood to be an equal-opportunity destroyer, but it was not. The water discriminated violently against the predominantly African American poor population of New Orleans whose neighborhoods were located in the lowest lying areas. Worse, the poor had no means to evacuate and could not escape the devastated city. As the folks with cars and a place to go fled to higher ground, thousands of poor people, mostly African Americans, were left behind to face the deluge, the deprivation, and the chaos.

The poor have never been on a level field with the middle class or wealthy. In the United States—as around the world—floods, famine, and even lesser disasters, such as family discord or illness, impose harsher effects on the poor than on the wealthy. We were not all born to equal circumstances. Life is not fair. Even so, as Americans watched the aftermath of the New Orleans flood, they were disturbed by the images of inequality. They cringed as they were reminded of the chasm between rich and poor, black and white. After all, America aspires to something greater. Although American democracy does not require economic equality, it does require equal civil and political rights and "equal opportunity." This is supposed to be the "land of opportunity."

The chosen American *method* of providing opportunity is the public school. The public schools, from their founding, were hailed as "the great equalizer of the conditions of men—the balance-wheel of the social machinery" (Mann [1848] 1947, 86). Horace Mann ([1848] 1957) explained:

> If one class possesses all the wealth and the education, while the residue of society is ignorant and poor, it matters not by what name the relation between them may be called; the latter, in fact and in truth, will be the servile dependents and subjects of the former. But if education be equably diffused, it will draw prop-

erty after it, by the strongest of all attractions; for such a thing never did happen, and never can happen, as that an intelligent and practical body of men should be permanently poor. (87)

Although this ideal is theoretically appealing, its practical implementation has faced tremendous obstacles. Mann's vision of education as a social balance-wheel was not and is not shared by many of the advocates and consumers of public education. Self-interest and the desire to perpetuate privilege compete mightily with the distributive ideal. Further, distributing education equally has proved to be a difficult task, even when there is the political will to support it. The nation's poor and ethnic and racial minorities have engaged in more than a century of struggle to gain access to equal opportunity in education, but the gap between the educational "haves" and "have nots" persists. In school resources and in student academic achievement, the gap between rich and poor, minority and majority, endures.

Two recent books explore contemporary efforts to close the education gap. In *Final Test: The Battle for Adequacy in America's Schools*, Peter Schrag chronicles ongoing efforts to enlist the power of the courts to effect equal educational opportunity through court-ordered remedies. Richard Rothstein, in *Class and Schools: Using Social, Economic and Educational Reform to Close the Black-White Achievement Gap*, looks to social science and to educational and social reform for potential solutions to the problem. Both books provide an enriched, scholarly background for considering the problem of providing an equal education in an unequal society.

Final Test picks up the story of the pursuit of equal educational opportunity as the legal battle for reform moved from the federal to the state courts. Decades after the Supreme Court's landmark ruling in *Brown v. Board of Education*, advocates for poor and minority children needed a new strategy. Years of desegregation lawsuits following *Brown* had reached a dead end. Hopes that the federal court might require states to equalize educational spending for children in rich and poor districts were dashed by the Supreme Court's ruling in *San Antonio v. Rodriguez* in 1973, which held that public education was not a right guaranteed by the U.S. Constitution. Meanwhile, the public schools remained substantially racially segregated and savagely unequal. (Orfield 2001; Frankenberg and Lee 2002). Legal advocates began to look to state constitutional law as the source of the right to an education.

The first wave of lawsuits brought under state constitutional law sought equity in school funding. These suits encountered intense resistance from groups who feared that equalizing school finances would require "leveling down" resources available to schools in wealthy areas. Further, equal funding might be unattainable or even undesirable in light of the different conditions in existing schools and the differing needs of children in those schools. In the process of trying to fit the legal remedy to the *needs* of the children, advocates for poor children developed a new strategy around the concept of an "adequate" education. The adequacy strategy was pushed forward, in part, by the standards movement, which had resulted in educational standards being articulated and adopted in almost every state (82). After all, the reasoning goes, if states are going to hold school children accountable to certain standards before they are allowed to graduate, then the state should be held equally accountable to provide the resources to enable the children to meet those standards (247). Adequacy lawsuits seek revenues and resources based on calculations of what it actually takes—in teachers, books, facilities, and other resources—to educate each child to state standards.

In the tradition of *Simple Justice* (Kluger 1975), the classic history of *Brown v. Board of Education,* Peter Schrag tells the story of the adequacy lawsuits, introducing us to the people behind the litigation and providing the context for the suits and the reasons for the strategies chosen. He chronicles legal battles in Kentucky, California, New Jersey, Ohio, Alabama, North Carolina, Maryland, and New York. In doing so, he condenses decades of legal argument and volumes of court opinions into readable stories—and at the same time is faithful to the legal details of the litigation. Without using legal jargon, Schrag accurately and cogently captures the process and the legal meaning of court opinions. In a few instances Schrag introduces us to the participants in the legal drama. For example, in chapter 1 Schrag illuminates the conditions in one California school through Alondra Jones, a high school student, who tells us, "It makes you feel less about yourself, you know, like you sitting here in a class where you have to stand up because there's not enough chairs, and you see rats in the buildings, the bathrooms is nasty ... " (21). In chapter 3, we hear the expert witness for the plaintiffs, John Augenblick, recoil after an unpleasant experience on the witness stand, saying, "This isn't supposed to be a murder trial. [But] the lawyers do everything they can to win" (136).

Most of the story, however, is told at the level of political wrangling and court opinion. Schrag shows us that legal rights are not pristine concepts within the court's power. It seems that almost everyone—legislators, teachers' associations, business organizations, governors, taxpayers, parents, and students—has a stake in school finance litigation and all expect to have a degree of control over the outcome. The political self-interests of governors, legislators, and elected judges weigh heavily in the balance against requiring taxpayers to support new appropriations for schools in poor areas. Meanwhile, as litigation is ongoing, the school systems function on yearly appropriations. Gains made in one year can be erased in the next. Further, new appropriations—when they do come—are sometimes subject to mismanagement and corruption at the school and district levels. Even state supreme courts alternately exercise their power in favor of the rights of poor students and then back off again under the political pressure that follows controversial court opinions. In Ohio and Alabama, for example, the supreme courts flip-flopped on school finance issues and ultimately abdicated any role whatsoever in enforcing constitutional standards enunciated in previous rulings (142, 151).

Schrag's account of the equity-adequacy litigation chronicles a prolonged power struggle among branches of government and elements of society over resources. Although adequacy suits attempt to "integrate educational practice with finance," (247) money is the central issue. On that issue, Schrag counts adequacy suits as a partial success, with momentum building toward even greater success. Despite decades-long court battles that have produced ambiguous legal results, Schrag is cautiously optimistic. He points to increased per-pupil spending—which has risen dramatically since 1990—and the decrease in funding disparities between rich and poor schools apparent in states like Ohio, Kentucky, and New Jersey (243). In chapter 4, however, Schrag acknowledges that adequacy suits sidestep the thorny question: Does money matter? In other words, adequacy suits assume that providing better resources to poor schools will improve the academic achievement of the students in those schools. But what if that is not the case? What if new spending on schools does not yield expected gains in student achievement? What if providing adequate resources does not close the achievement gap between rich and poor, minority and majority? Schrag's answer to this question is that schools will not resolve all of society's problems but that they are the best option we have. We have to try to provide each child with a meaningful educational opportunity, says Schrag, because schools are our "great democratic equalizer" (248). Schrag concludes that we must summon all of our political will to provide adequate schools because there is no other choice if we are ever to achieve the "great promises of American society: equality, opportunity and human and social betterment" (249).

Schrag's final questions are the jumping off point for Richard Rothstein's book, *Class and Schools.* In contrast to Schrag, Rothstein does not expect increased school funding or school reform of any kind to close the achievement gap between rich and poor, minority and majority. Instead, he argues that "the influence of social class characteristics is probably so powerful that schools cannot overcome it, no matter how well trained are their teachers and no matter how well designed are their instructional programs and climates" (5). Rothstein contends that social class, which he defines as "a collection of occupational, psychological, personality, health, and economic traits that interact," is a powerful predictor of academic and occupational success (4). Further, he says, cultural characteristics—"for example, [that] black students may value education less than white students because a discriminatory labor market has not historically rewarded black workers for their education"—play an important role in perpetuating the black-white achievement gap (4). According to Rothstein, raising the achievement of "lower-class" children will require social and economic reform not just school reform (11).

Rothstein's book presents a wide-ranging critique of schools and society. He begins by examining the reasons for the existence of the achievement gap in standardized test scores, including genetics, poor health care, unstable housing, and "cultural" differences. Having shown that the problems lower class children face are broad and deep, Rothstein goes on to critique the idea that the gap can be closed by following the practices that have been successful in a few exceptional schools. Each of those schools, he says, succeeded and thrived because of a cluster of factors that are not generalizable or repeatable. He then argues that another gap—a social class gap in noncognitive skills like persistence, motivation, and reliability—is even more important than the gap in literacy and numeracy. Finally, he suggests a list of reforms that could narrow the achievement gap, including raising the minimum wage; helping poor families with children find stable housing; creating school-community clinics; and providing early childhood education, summer programs, and after-school programs.

Rothstein's strongest and most intuitive argument is that if children's lives are improved, their school performance will improve. This point seems self-evident but bears repeating. Rothstein points to studies that show how disparities in health care and housing adversely affect the academic achievement of poor children. He argues, for example, that one of the most efficient ways to narrow the achievement gap would be to provide poor children with vision screening and appropriate glasses (37–38). Other academic gains would be realized if poor children had stable housing; dental and medical care; proper nutrition; protection from lead dust exposure; and protection from prenatal exposure to alcohol, tobacco, and drugs.

Rothstein's other arguments are weakened by his use of "class" and "culture." Rothstein contends that using the term class is superior to using euphemisms like "disadvantaged" students or "at risk" students because the term lower class captures both economic and cultural characteristics that go beyond a single year's poverty (3–4). He points out that a single year of low family income does not accurately predict which children are likely to be on the low end of the achievement gap. The child of a Yale graduate student may have a low income in a given year but will have other advantages that most poor children do not have. Poverty measures, he claims, are inadequate to capture the "collection of characteristics" and culture that define lower class. Unfortunately, however, Rothstein does not explain what the collection of characteristics that define lower class is. As I read, I become suspicious that they are, in fact, based on stereotypes and little data. This book, which depends on data for many of its claims, neglects to give us any data or evaluation of the existence of an identifiable lower class. By giving short shrift to his definition of class, and by attributing negative cultural qualities to this inartfully constructed class, Rothstein runs the risk of perpetuating social stereotypes and negative attitudes about poor people.

It is also troubling that Rothstein slips back and forth between discussing issues of class and culture and discussing the "black-white achievement gap." In reality, the children who are likely to come to school with educational deficits, the ones who are likely to be on the low end of the achievement gap, include children who come from families living in chronic poverty, living in areas of concentrated poverty, or belonging to a racial or ethnic group that has suffered historical and continuing discrimination. These children come from diverse cultures—Native American, Appalachian, African American, Cajun, Hispanic, and others. We know that a disproportionate number of African Americans live in chronic or concentrated poverty (Rusk 1999; McArdle 2003), but even greater numbers (but a smaller percentage) of white children also live in chronic or concentrated poverty—and suffer similar learning challenges (DeNavas-Walt et al. 2005).

The separation of children into neighborhood schools—poor schools in poor neighborhoods and wealthy schools in wealthy neighborhoods—perpetuates privilege for some and lower class status for others. The concentration of poverty in certain neighborhoods and certain schools compounds all of the problems that Rothstein so carefully documents. However, no child deserves to be labeled "lower class" or to receive a lower class education. Each child deserves a first class education. The promise of the common school movement and of *Brown v. Board of Education* was that children would go to school—rich, poor, black, white, Hispanic, Native American—together. When poor and minority children escape schools where poverty is concentrated, their academic achievement improves. Although Rothstein acknowledges this phenomenon, he claims that "we Americans are apparently unwilling to consider the housing, transportation, zoning and other urban policies that would permit families of different classes to live in close proximity so their children can attend the same neighborhood schools" (130).

Despite Rothstein's assertion, there are some school districts that integrate students of different income levels and racial groups. Raleigh, North Carolina, for example, transports children out of their neighborhoods to ensure that no school has more than 40 percent poor children (Finder 2005). Even so, Rothstein, if he chose to, could cite good evidence to support his pessimism about the probability of change. Many Americans prefer their separate and unequal schools. Those in power, the wealthy, the elite, like their privileges and advantages. Of course they do. The problem is not only a problem of inequality but also a problem of persuasion. No social or educational reform can be effective without the support of those who live above the poverty line and do not suffer from racial or ethnic discrimination. When well-off citizens are convinced that preventing or ameliorating child poverty is in their interest, they can be persuaded to support social reforms. When well-off citizens are convinced that child poverty increases social dysfunction domestically and decreases competitiveness internationally, they can be persuaded to support social reform. When well-off citizens are persuaded that the gap in educational quality does not serve our society well, when they realize that the cost of low-quality education is extraordinarily high, they see that equitable, adequate, and integrated schools are worth the investment.

Even when support for social and educational reform is strong, however, the necessity of new persuasion is constant. Backsliding is a perennial threat (Lee 2004). Annually, a new group of children enter school. The needs of these children are just as great as the needs of the children who came into school a year or a generation before. The well-off must be persuaded year after year after year to part with their money for the benefit of the greater social good. How much easier it is to segregate the problems of race and poverty into separate schools! How convenient to forget about them.

It took a hurricane and the flooding of New Orleans to remind some Americans that the poor are hit harder by every disaster and have less ability to escape. It took a hurricane to remind some Americans that we live in an unequal society where some groups have built their homes above sea level and other groups are concentrated in low-lying areas. In an unequal society, the task of creating equal or adequate educational opportunity for all children is much like protecting a city built below sea level: It requires a constant effort to hold back the sea—and a whole lot of pumping. It is an enormous task. *The Final Test* and *Class and Schools* urge us to keep working.

References

DeNavas-Walt, Carmen, Bernadette D. Proctor, and Cheryl H. Lee. 2005. *Income, Poverty, and Health Insurance Coverage in the United States: 2004.* U.S. Census Bureau Current Population Report. P60–229. Washington, D.C.: U.S. Government Printing Office.

Finder, Alan. 2005. "As Test Scores Jump, Raleigh Credits Integration by Income." *The New York Times,* 25 September, A1.

Frankenberg, Erica, and Chungmei Lee. 2002. *Race in American Public Schools: Rapidly Resegregating School Districts.* http://www.civilrightsproject.harvard.edu/research/deseg/Race_in_American_Public_Schools1.p df

Kluger, Richard. 1975. *Simple Justice: The History of Brown v. Board of Education and Black America's Struggle for Equality.* New York: Knopf.

Lee, Chungmei. 2004. *Is Resegregation Real?* http://www.civilrightsproject.harvard.edu/research/reseg03/mumford_response.php

Mann, Horace. [1848] 1957. *Twelfth Annual Report of the Board of Education, Together with the Annual Report of the Secretary of the Board, 1837–1848.* Reprinted in *The Republic and the School* 84–91 (Lawrence A. Cremin, ed.) New York: Teachers College, Columbia University.

McArdle, Nancy. 2003. *Beyond Poverty: Race and Concentrated-Poverty Neighborhoods in Metro Boston.* http://www.civilrightsproject.harvard.edu/research/metro/poverty_boston.php

Orfield, Gary. 2001. *Schools More Separate: Consequences of a Decade of Resegregation.* http://www.civilrightsproject.harvard.edu/research/deseg/separate_schools01.php

Rusk, David. 1999. *Inside Game/Outside Game: Winning Strategies for Saving Urban America.* Washington, D.C.: Brookings Institution Press.

Savage Inequalities: Children in America's Schools.

Jonathan Kozol. New York: Crown, 1991. 262 pp. $14.00 (paper).

RAQUEL L. FARMER-HINTON
University of Wisconsin-Milwaukee

Fifteen years ago, Jonathan Kozol's *Savage Inequalities: Children in America's Schools* exposed vast educational disparities between schools attended by the affluent and the poor, and by white children and children of color, which shocked scholars and practitioners into the grim reality of schooling inequalities in the United States. *Savage Inequalities* became one of our most widely discussed books because it ignited a moral outrage about the absence of educational opportunity for students of color from poor communities while the privileged educational opportunities of their white and affluent counterparts were secured through school funding formulas. In this retrospective review, I discuss the significance of this seminal book. I provide an overview of Kozol's indictment against equal educational opportunity in the United States, discuss the impact of *Savage Inequalities* on the money matters debate, and then explore Kozol's foresight about the long-term consequences of educational inequalities.

Rhetoric Versus Painted Realities

Kozol critiques the American ideal of equal educational opportunity by juxtaposing our rhetoric with the daily realities of students of color from poor communities. From rainwater in classrooms to inadequate heating and ventilation, from falling paint chips and concrete to poorly functioning restrooms, and from overcrowded classrooms to faulty cafeterias, Kozol's vivid descriptions of these students' victimization are palpable. He condemns the inconsistency between our espoused principles and the horrifying conditions in which many students are forced to learn. More importantly, he condemns the double standards that limits educational opportunities for students of color from poor communities and allows unlimited educational opportunities for their white and affluent counterparts:

> The crowding of children into insufficient, often squalid spaces seems an inexplicable anomaly in the United States. Images of spaciousness and majesty, of endless plains and soaring mountains, fill our folklore and our music and the anthems that our children sing. "This land is your land," they are told; and, in one of the patriotic songs that children truly love because it summons up so well the goodness and the optimism of the nation at its best, they sing of "good" and "brotherhood" "from sea to shining sea." It is a betrayal of the best things that we

value when poor children are obliged to sing these songs in storerooms and coat closets. (160)

Kozol issues his indictment against our ideal of equal educational opportunity by critiquing our school finance structure, which deliberately disenfranchises students of color from poor communities. Kozol bases his indictment on the systemic educational inequalities fostered from the large variability in local property wealth. He notes that the fiscal challenges in the East St. Louis school system, for example, did not occur in isolation, as there were other communities he visited in Illinois, New York, New Jersey, Texas, and Washington, D.C. where community wealth dictated students' opportunities to learn:

> In suburban Millburn, where per-pupil spending is some $1500 more than in East Orange although the tax rate in East Orange is three times as high, 14 different AP [Advanced Placement] courses are available to high school students; the athletic program offers fencing, golf, ice hockey and lacrosse; and music instruction means ten music teachers. (157)

In addition to many of the aforementioned problems with building age and infrastructure, Kozol found other systemic problems like teacher shortages, which occurred disproportionately in poorer districts because funding differentials impacted teachers' salaries and working conditions (see also Darling-Hammond and Green 1990; Ferguson 1991; Oakes 1990). Principals and administrators noted how they could not compete with higher-salaried and higher-resourced schools so many of their talented teachers left after getting enough experience to compete for positions in affluent school systems. As a result, schools serving poor students of color were more likely to have vacancies that, if filled, were filled with substitute teachers or teachers without credentials in their subject area:

> The problems are systemic: The number of teachers over 60 years of age in the Chicago system is twice that of the teachers under 30. The salary scale, too low to keep exciting, youthful teachers in the system, leads the city to rely on low-paid subs, who represent more than a quarter of Chicago's teaching force ... . But even substitute teachers in Chicago are quite frequently in short supply. On an average morning in Chicago, 5,700 children in 190 classrooms come to school to find they have no teacher. (52)

Additionally, without appropriate funding levels, Kozol found that poor schools disproportionately offered a narrower curriculum. For example, an affluent school in Cherry Hill, New Jersey, offered fourteen physical science courses and eighteen biology electives, and its neighboring schools struggled to provide the minimum of science course offerings. Moreover, even if advanced courses were present in the curriculum, poor schools lacked the teachers, books, instructional resources, and appropriate class sizes to implement an advanced curriculum (see also Consortium for Policy Research in Education 1991). Kozol reports:

> The biology lab, which I visit next, has no laboratory table. Students work at regular desks. "I need dissecting kits," the teacher says. "The few we have are incomplete." Chemical supplies, she tells me, in a city poisoned by two chemical plants, are scarce. "I need more microscopes," she adds. The chemistry lab is the only one that's properly equipped. There are eight lab tables with gas jets and water. But the chemistry teacher says he rarely brings his students to the lab. "I have 30 children in a class and cannot supervise them safely. Chemical lab work is unsafe with more than 20 children to a teacher. If I had some lab assistants, we could make use of the lab. As it is, we have to study mainly from a text." (28)

As Kozol's audience, we found it difficult to fathom how these kinds of injustices could exist in American schools especially when bordering school communities had an abundance of resources. When I read *Savage Inequalities* in college, I found Kozol's descriptions eerily familiar. When he visited East St. Louis, Illinois, in the late 1980s, I was attending a local high school, which suffered from many of the problems described in his first chapter, such as missing or inadequate science equipment and curricula, poor sports facilities, and a school library made inoperable from a city flood. As a high school student, my first attempt at activism was complaining about faulty toilets and missing toilet paper. After reading *Savage Inequalities*, I realized I was naïve about the source of my frustration. Kozol's work was powerful because it taught me (as well as other readers) that students' limited access to school resources was the result of inequality by design.[1]

Savage Inequalities and the Money Matters Debate

Savage Inequalities expanded our knowledge of why and how money matters to students' academic outcomes. *The Coleman Report* (1966) ignited "the money matters debate" because it was the most noted study to address whether variations in school resources existed among schools, particularly between schools that were predominantly white and predominantly of color. The report documented inequalities but found little relationship to student achievement. In fact, the study concluded that inequalities existing in homes, neighborhoods, and peer environments (not schools) accounted for most of the variations in student test scores (Coleman et al. 1966). The report satisfied political conservatives because there was no longer a justification for equalizing school funding.

After *The Coleman Report*, the money matters debate became a contentious arena for conceptual and methodological discussions because the idea that money did not matter lacked intuitive sense (Armor 1972). Spady (1976) argued that school effect studies, such as *The Coleman Report* and other noted studies like Jencks' *Inequality* (1972), had methodological and substantive flaws, which diminished the relationship between expenditures and student achievement. As the debate progressed, many studies found positive effects of money and resources on student achievement (see Bowles 1977; Childs and Shakeshaft 1986; Ginsburg, Moskowitz, and Rosenthal 1981; Guthrie, Kleindorfer, Levin, and Stout 1971; Hartman 1988; Kirst 1983; Sebold and Dato 1981; Verstegen and Salmon 1989; Wendling and Cohen 1981). However, Hanushek's (1989) meta-analysis resounded that expenditures and resources (particularly teacher-student ratios, teacher's educational background, teacher experience, teacher salaries, expenditures per pupil, and administrative expenditures) were not consistently related to student performance.

Savage Inequalities enters the money matters debate at this juncture to fill an important gap in the literature. First, Kozol uses qualitative methods to examine the relationship between money and students' schooling experiences and outcomes. His classroom observations as well as student and staff interviews provide a rich account of the effect of limited funding on the organizational capacity of schools. From his classroom observation notes and staff interviews, he conveys how additional dollars could improve building infrastructure, curricular content, and instruction. He interviewed students and used their voices to share their daily experiences in and perceptions of their poorly funded schools as well as the negative impact on their school attachment and academic performance. Kozol's use of qualitative methods deepens our clarity on the impact of poor school funding on the organizational capacity of schools. More importantly, his approach focuses us on the important stakeholders in this whole genre of work.

Second, Kozol expands our notion of how to measure the impact of money on students' learning experiences. He demonstrates how resources extend beyond the presence of exemplary teachers and enriched curricula to students' utility and access to those resources—unlike many studies, such as *The Coleman Report*, that analyzed only administrative counts and records of the presence of resources and their impact on student outcomes (see Smith 1972). The distinction is grounded in the manner in which Kozol explores, for example, how two neighboring high schools both had science laboratories, but the laboratories were not equally accessible to students, that is, in good working condition and accompanied by a curriculum and instructor to ensure proper use.

Lastly, Kozol expands our conceptual clarity of how money impacts students' schooling experiences. Kozol explains the concept of money as purchasing power, whereas wealthier school districts had the fiscal capabilities (due to local property values) of exercising their purchasing power to acquire quality personnel and resources, poorer school districts could not afford the "bare necessities" (33). Additionally, the reputations of wealthier school districts helped to create a competitive market for neighborhood homes, which further increased property values and helped them garner more luxuries for their student populations. Kozol also notes that the purchasing power of wealthier districts included not only their fiscal capabilities but also their power to attract resources to their school communities by providing a compensation package with nonmonetary benefits such as newer facilities, up-to-date equipment, and smaller class sizes. Thus, their purchasing power often pulled resources from poorer districts (see also Darling-Hammond and Green 1990; Ferguson 1991; Oakes 1990).

The Savage-ness of the Cost

In *Savage Inequalities*, Kozol shares the long-term consequences of educational inequalities to both individuals and whole school communities. He discusses the immense cost placed on students who attend a compulsory school system that deliberately fosters an "unequal contest" (180). Throughout the book, Kozol explores the existence of two distinct learning experiences—one for poor students of color to occupy semiskilled jobs and one for white and affluent students to occupy white-collar jobs. Kozol alludes to the educational system's role in fostering a rigid caste system because (1) local wealth dictates school quality, (2) quality schools dictate students' access to resources that impact their performance and attainment, and (3) students' performance and attainment dictate financial rewards that allow access to homes in wealthier communities:

> In effect, a circular phenomenon evolves: The richer districts—those in which the property lots and houses are more highly valued—have more revenue, derived from taxing land and homes, to fund their public schools. The reputation of the schools, in turn, adds to the value of their homes, and this, in turn, expands the tax base for their public schools. The fact that they can levy lower taxes than the poorer districts, but exact more money, raises values even more; and this, again, means further funds for smaller classes and for higher teacher salaries within their public schools. Few of the children in the schools of Roosevelt or Mount Vernon will, as a result, be likely to compete effectively with kids in Great Neck and Manhasset for admissions to the better local colleges and universities of New York state ... and few of the graduates or dropouts of those poorer systems, as a consequence, are likely ever to earn enough to buy a home in Great Neck or Manhasset. (121)

Kozol finds it particularly troublesome that these dual educational systems were supported by policymakers, business owners, and suburban citizens based on their "conservative anxiety" (172) that equalizing school funding could dispossess wealthier districts of their luxuries, although those fears were often couched in a language of poor school districts being "black holes" where money cannot produce improved student outcomes (53). Moreover, he points out the irony of our willingness to blame poorly educated adults for their social and economic circum-stances, while forgetting "what we did to her when she was eight years old in ele-mentary school or 15 years old at DuSable High" in Chicago (73).

Kozol also helps us understand the immense cost placed on poor school com-munities. He notes that the fiscal challenges in many school communities com-pound over time. Kozol warns us about educational vestiges when he quotes a prin-cipal saying, in each successive school year, "there's one more toilet that doesn't flush, one more drinking fountain that doesn't work, one more classroom without texts" (37). Additionally, Kozol points out the unfairness of increasing school ac-countability measures while enduring fiscal challenges weaken school capacities. Kozol suggests there is "failure by design" when policymakers put the onus of ad-dressing the achievement gap on poorly funded schools (145). He explains that schools' reform efforts do not offer a real opportunity for change unless adequate financial support is provided:

> In the education catch-up game, we are entrapped by teaching to the tests. In keeping with the values of these recent years, the state requires test results. It "mandates" higher scores. But it provides us no resources in the areas that count to make this possible. So it is a rather hollow "mandate" after all, as if you could create these things by shouting at the wind …. What is the result? We are prepar-ing a generation of robots. Kids are learning exclusively through rote. We have children who are given no conceptual framework. They do not learn to think be-cause their teachers are straightjacketed by tests that measure only isolated skills. (143)

In summary, *Savage Inequalities* offers a profound analysis of the winners and losers in the U.S. school system. The book is powerful because it arouses a "heightened bitterness" by juxtaposing schools in poor communities of color against the schools in white and more affluent neighborhoods (74). Kozol's schol-arship ignites a fervent dialogue about our vacuous ideals and the subsequent im-pact on the schooling experiences of poor students of color. However, despite Kozol's sharp polemic for us to address educational inequality, there have not been fundamental changes to school funding disparities (Hussar and Sonnenberg 2000). Ironically, our accountability measures have increased for those schools already weakened by vestiges of poor school funding. In East St. Louis, Illinois, for exam-ple, only 32 percent of students meet or exceed state standards.[2] Realistically, how can a district with decades of a weakened tax base gain the purchasing power to improve students' test scores? Our retrospective review of *Savage Inequalities* re-minds us that our empty ideals have endured because current reforms mask old eq-uity issues while the true promise of educational opportunity rests with revising the school finance structure.

Notes

1. I must acknowledge that I had more privileges within the East St. Louis school system than most of my peers. Although Kozol painted a vivid picture of the challenges in East St. Louis and its school system, he did not discuss the variations in our class structure. As one of those privileged few, my background and family connections gave me access to the best resources that the East St. Louis school system could offer while students without those connections lacked the same opportunities.
2. The State of Illinois produces school report cards on all schools within the state. There is also an interactive version of their system, which aggregates school report cards to the district level (http://iirc.niu.edu).

References

Armor, David J. 1972. "School and Family Effects on Black and White Achievement: A Reexamination of USOE Data." In *On Equality of Educational Opportunity,* edited by Frederick Mosteller, and Daniel P. Moynihan, 168–229. New York: Random House.
Bowles, Samuel. 1977. "Unequal Education and the Reproduction of the Social Division of Labor." In *Power and Ideology in Education,* edited by Jerome Karabel and Albert H. Halsey, 137–153. New York: Oxford University Press.
Childs, T. Stephen, and Charol Shakeshaft. 1986. "A Meta-Analysis of Research on the Relationship Between Educational Expenditures and Student Achievement." *Journal of Education Finance* 12:249–263.
Coleman, James S., et al. 1966. *Equality of Educational Opportunity.* Washington, D.C.: U.S. Government Printing Office.
Consortium for Policy Research in Education. 1991. *Equality in Education: Progress, Problems, and Possibilities.* New Brunswick, NJ: CPRE.
Darling-Hammond, Linda, and Joslyn Green. 1990. "Teacher Quality and Equality." In *Access to Knowledge: An Agenda for Our Nation's Schools,* edited by John I. Goodlad and Pamela Keating, 237–258. New York: College Entrance Examination Board.
Ferguson, Ronald L. 1991. "Paying for Public Education: New Evidence on How and Why Money Matters." *Harvard Journal on Legislation* 28:465–491.
Ginsburg, Alan, Jay H. Moskowitz, and Alvin S. Rosenthal. 1981. "A School Based Analysis of Inter- and Intradistrict Resource Allocation." *Journal of Education Finance* 6:440–455.
Guthrie, James W., et al. 1971. *Schools and Inequality.* Cambridge: The Massachusetts Institute of Technology Press.
Hanushek, Eric. 1989. "The Impact of Differential Expenditures on School Performance." *Educational Researcher* 18:45–51, 62.
Hartman, William T. 1988. "District Spending Disparities: What Do the Dollars Buy?" *Journal of Education Finance* 13:436–459.
Hussar, William, and William Sonnenberg. 2000. *Trends in Disparities in School District Level Expenditures Per Pupil.* Washington, D.C.: National Center for Education Statistics.
Jencks, Christopher. 1972. *Inequality: A Reassessment of the Effect of Family and Schooling in America.* New York: Basic Books.
Kirst, Michael W. 1983. "A New School Finance for a New Era of Fiscal Constraint." ERIC Document Reproduction Service No. ED 235 565.
Oakes, Jeannie. 1990. *Multiplying Inequalities: The Effects of Race, Social Class, and Tracking on Opportunities to Learn Mathematics and Science.* Santa Monica, Calif.: The RAND Corporation.
Sebold, Frederick D., and William Dato. 1981. "School Funding and Student Achievement: An Empirical Analysis." *Public Finance Quarterly* 9:91–105.

Smith, Marshall. 1972. "Equality of Educational Opportunity: The Basic Findings Reconsidered." In *On Equality Of Educational Opportunity,* edited by Frederick Mosteller and Daniel P. Moynihan, 168–229. New York: Random House.

Spady, W. 1976. The Impact of Social Resources on Students. In *School and Achievement in American Society,* edited by W. H. Sewell, R. M. Hauser & D. L. Featherman. New York: Academic Press.

Verstegen, Deborah A., and Richard G. Salmon. 1989. "The Conceptualization and Measurement of Equity in School Finance in Virginia." *Journal of Education Finance* 15:205–228.

Wendling, Wayne, and Judith Cohen. 1981. "Education Resources and Student Achievement: Good News for Schools." *Journal of Education Finance* 7:44–63.

Reflections on the Moral and Spiritual Crisis in Education. David E. Purpel and William M. McLaurin, Jr. New York: Peter Lang, 2004. 298 pp. $29.95 (paper).

SABRINA ROSS
The University of North Carolina at Greensboro

Can we create a society in which education is conceived of in its broadest context as the search for meaning and purpose? What is the role of the educator in the realization of such a society? How can an educational philosophy grounded in wisdom and spirituality encourage the creation of a socially just world community? David Purpel and William McLaurin, Jr. address these and other questions relevant to transformative education in their ambitious project, *Reflections on the Moral and Spiritual Crisis in Education.*

The book provides theory and methodology for educational transformation guided by spiritual practice. The book articulates an educational philosophy and curriculum based on human dignity, meaning, and purpose. The authors' goal is to transform an oppressive culture through the realization of a more just and loving world community. Certainly, concepts such as spirituality, human dignity, and love seem ill-placed within the context of our present educational discourse. *Reflections on the Moral and Spiritual Crisis in Education* emphasizes a radical transformation of the existing educational system, which, the authors argue, is an insufficient enterprise for pursuing meaning, fulfillment, and purpose.

Reflections on the Moral and Spiritual Crisis in Education is comprised of two books. The first, *The Moral and Spiritual Crisis in Education,* is a reprint in its entirety (with minor editing) of Purpel's 1989 book of the same title. Book I offers a critique of the lack of moral significance attached to education. The second book, *Reflections on the Moral and Spiritual Crisis in Education,* discusses recent changes in education and society (e.g., terrorist attacks of 9/11, No Child Left Behind mandates, and globalization) and the impact of these changes on the American educational system. Additionally, Book II provides a restructured argument for the educational philosophy espoused in Book I.

In chapter 1, "The Current Crisis in Education," Purpel establishes a relationship between education and culture and argues that our society is in the midst of a cultural crisis that has produced an educational crisis. Chapter two, "Recent Educational Reform," is a deconstruction of mainstream educational discourse. In this chapter, Purpel discusses what he identifies as the reification of education—an illusory separation of education from a larger moral context that results in a highly technical and ultimately trivial educational system. A recurring theme of chapters one and two is the need to conceive of education within a moral framework as a search for purpose and meaning.

"The Moral and Spiritual Crisis in American Education," the third chapter of Book I, discusses the conflicting moral beliefs that are espoused in mainstream American culture. For Purple, these unresolved moral conflicts act as roadblocks to educational equity and social justice. The author suggests that a unifying mythos—an internally consistent, overarching belief system derived from a moral and spiritual framework—is needed for educational transformation.

Chapter 4, "A Religious and Moral Framework for American Education," offers a mythos based on an eclectic construction of theologies (liberation and creation) and philosophic traditions (Socratic and prophetic) for educational and cultural transformation. A central theme of this chapter is prophecy, defined as that which "holds us to our deepest commitments, chides us when we do not meet them, and provides hope for us when we think we cannot" (5). Purpel repeatedly emphasizes distinctions between his use of the construct of spirituality (an order of reality not grounded in materialism) and institutionalized versions of religion. He argues that the latter tends toward narrow views and exclusion, while the former is based on an espoused sacredness of all humanity that is fundamentally inclusive in nature.

"Education in a Prophetic Voice," the fifth chapter of Book I, argues that life, when unconnected to sources of ultimate meaning, breeds cynicism and despair. This chapter also offers a conceptualization of the educator as prophet and discusses how educators can overcome the despair that hinders social transformation by embracing the prophetic—the search for ultimate meaning through simultaneous processes of criticism, creativity, and imagination.

Chapter 6 of Book I, "A Curriculum for Social Justice and Compassion," presents goals and objectives for a social justice curriculum. Essential aspects of Purpel's curriculum are criticality in consciousness of history, criticality in the accumulation of knowledge, social skills (e.g., community building), cultural competence, cultural consciousness, and a unifying mythos. The final chapter of Book I, "Issues of Curriculum Planning, Design, and Implementation," addresses the difficulty of implementing this radical plan of educational transformation. Resistance, sabotage, and co-optation are discussed along with the author's assessment of the feasibility of this project. The chapter also describes actual projects approximating Purpel's vision of a social justice curriculum.

In light of what the authors perceive as decidedly negative turns in education since the 1989 publication of The *Moral and Spiritual Crisis in Education*—overly politicized educational reform initiatives, social curricula of competition and privilege, and a highly controlled community of professional educators—Purpel and McLaurin significantly revised arguments set forth in Book I in Book II, *Reflections on the Moral and Spiritual Crisis in Education.*

Chapter 1, "That Was Then and This Is Now: The Deepening Educational and Cultural Crisis," suggests a new and more pressing crisis now exists in American culture in general and in the educational system in particular because consumerism, globalization, and the dominance of western culture have exacerbated the effects of an educational system based on economic logic rather than social justice. Purpel and McLaurin retain their original argument for the fundamentally moral nature of the educational crisis in the United States but place greater emphasis on the role of spirituality in educational transformation. Whereas Book I implies that one can use either a moral or spiritual framework as a source of sustenance for attaining social justice, Purpel and McLaurin conclude in Book II that a spiritual framework is prerequisite for the radical educational transformation they seek. The authors argue that radical transformation in education and society requires a fundamental change in humanity that cannot be achieved solely through appeals to critical consciousness or moral sensibilities. For Purpel and McLaurin, only a spiritual framework that "transforms the human participant in some profound sense for the better" is capable of preventing despair over the present educational crisis and sustaining a common mythos for educational transformation (221).

Chapter 2, "The Struggle for Moral and Spiritual Affirmation in an Age of Greed, Fanaticism, and Cynicism," is a very hopeful chapter. Here the authors share their belief that instances of social injustice are mainly produced through frustration and confusion rather than actual desires to oppress or cause harm to others. For Purpel and McLaurin, such belief is an essential aspect of their educational philosophy because it suggests that education can facilitate social justice by alleviating the frustration and confusion that cause oppression. Purple and McLaurin explain the necessity of their belief system as follows: "When we look at our problems as rooted in evil and sin, then the only alternative to despair is prayer; but when we are able to see them based more on confusion then we can put our hope in education" (195). This conceptualization is beneficial because it holds potential for transcending seemingly irreconcilable differences in our world community. For Purpel and McLaurin, when education is directed against confusion and misdirected frustration, opportunities for forgiveness and reconciliation become possible. Such education holds potential for building the community of justice, meaning, and purpose the authors advocate.

Chapter 3, "The Need for Wisdom in an Age of Uncertainty and Skepticism," posits a relationship between spirituality, wisdom, and educational transformation. The authors explicate the concept of wisdom and argue that it allows discernment between inclusive spiritual grounding and exclusive institutionalized forms of religion. In the final two chapters of Book II, Purpel and McLaurin share their individual reflections on the role of wisdom in the pursuit of educational transformation.

In chapter 4, "A Response to the Crisis: The Quest for Wisdom in the Practice of Everyday Life," McLaurin argues that the unifying mythos needed for educational transformation will only be realized through wisdom gained from spiritual experience: "the hearing of one's heart" (230). McLaurin calls on educators to participate in the cultural repair that encourages educational environments of love, meaning, and justice. He charges educators with the responsibility of searching for a faith that energizes them and illumes a path for their learners. The spiritual path McLaurin describes reflects his belief that diverse religions, philosophies, and orientations can be part of a unifying mythos. Describing himself as agnostic, McLaurin describes aspects of Buddhist, Christian, Kabalist, Hindu, and Sufi traditions that have contributed to his spiritual path.

In the final chapter of Book II, "A Response to the Crisis: The Love of Wisdom and the Wisdom of Love," Purpel affirms a commitment to critical pedagogy through spiritually informed reflection, dialogue, and action. He again emphasizes the necessity of a spiritual grounding—"that which inspires and gives breath to" (268)—for directing and sustaining the work of educational transformation. Purpel argues that social change must occur prior to educational change. In Book I, Purpel suggests that educators, as social and moral change agents, should lead the charge toward educational transformation. Here, however, he argues that the repressive conditions under which most educators work makes it unlikely for educational transformation to occur before the social context needed for such transformation is achieved. Purpel therefore suggests that educators desirous of change involve themselves in larger cultural movements oriented toward social transformation in order to create the necessary conditions for educational transformation. Like McLaurin, in the preceding chapter, Purpel draws on aspects of his own spiritual path, comprised of the Jewish commitment to social justice and the rabbinic and prophetic traditions, to explicate the relationship between spirituality, wisdom, and educational transformation.

Reflections on the Moral and Spiritual Crisis in Education is not an optimistic book—it paints a bleak picture of an educational system moving ever farther away from democracy and justice. Yet this book is hopeful. Purpel and McLaurin provide an inclusive plan of educational transformation where virtually everyone is invited to critique, dialogue, create, and participate in changing the world. They successfully combine academic, moral, and spiritual language in a manner that is accessible to a wide audience. Educators who read this book will come away with a better understanding of the practice of critical pedagogy as well as a strong sense of their own agency in the monumental task of educational transformation.

This book will also be a useful for those currently revisiting Jonathan Kozol's (1991) *Savage Inequalities.* Whereas Kozol repeatedly questions the lack of moral outrage over the undemocratic treatment of youth in inner city public schools, Purpel and McLaurin explicate the social and historical antecedents of moral conflict that have resulted in a society that does not act in accord with its espoused democratic ideals. While *Savage Inequalities* may cause readers to despair over the lack of social justice for those marginalized and oppressed by the current educational system, *Reflections on the Moral and Spiritual Crisis in Education* provides much needed hope by emphasizing the power of human agency to effect change even under bleak and repressive circumstances.

ESSAY REVIEW

Report to the Minister: Review of the Financing, Resourcing and Costs of Education in Public Schools.

Published by the Department of Education, Pretoria, Republic of South Africa. Retieved May 10, 2006 from http://www.education.gov.za/dynamic.aspx?page id=329&catid=10&category=Reports.

LUIS CROUCH
Research Vice President, Research Triangle Institute, North Carolina

The document under discussion, published in 2003, is the first major self-assessment, by the democratic government, since 1994, of the postapartheid reforms of the funding of South Africa's public schools.[1] "The Report to the Minister: Review of the Financing, Resourcing and Costs of Education in Public Schools, Department of Education, South Africa" (hereafter "the Review") is a rich and detailed, book-length public sector self-review. There is much to be learned about South Africa's approach to education funding as well as from its approach to reviewing its own systems.

In order to understand such a document, however, it is vital to have some background on at least two issues: first, the situation during apartheid, and, second, the nature of the first wave of postapartheid reforms. It is only in this context that the report can make sense. In this note we thus first lay out some of this key background, before delving into the report itself. It is important to note that the author is not an impartial observer but was an actor, advising the government of South Africa on many of these reforms.[2] This review is then an "engaged" review, although the usual professional efforts to provide an objective view are, of course, made.

During apartheid, South Africa had one of the most unequal education systems on earth, if not the most unequal. Certainly, even today, the sequelae of apartheid are such that, of all countries participating in the "big" international assessments (Programme in International Student Assessment [PISA], Trends in International Mathematics and Science Study [TIMSS], Progress in International Reading Literacy Study [PIRLS]) and using the ratio of achievement at the ninety-fifth percentile of the distribution to achievement at the fifth percentile of the distribution, the internal inequality in South Africa is the highest of any measured country. The inequality was, of course, actively engineered. A few facts can be pointed out. First, white children had approximately ten times as many resources, per child, as the children in the poorest African "homeland." Pupil-teacher ratios for whites were about a third to a half that for African children. Teacher support in the white areas, in terms of the ratio of nonteaching staff to teaching staff, was approximately ten times as generous as in the poorest black areas, such as the KwaZulu homeland.

A few other interesting facts have to be born in mind. South Africa's education system was, and still is, overwhelmingly public. Ironically, only through private schools could African children receive a good education. Thus, many of the small minority of schools that were private were seen as quite progressive, both racially and pedagogically, and were able to integrate even during apartheid. These private schools had attracted much of the democratic African elite, and a historical debt of gratitude was felt to be owed them, to a significant degree, by key elements of this elite that then came to power in 1994. Nonetheless, the point is that because the system was dual and highly segregated, there had been no "white flight" to private schools, and private schools were a tiny minority of the system. South Africa was not, that is, similar to, say, the U.S. city, with its "white flight" (or "rich flight") to private schools.

Another important background factor was that South Africa had reached very high levels of coverage. Enrollment ratios at the primary level were actually way above 100 percent (because of overage and underage children) and at the secondary level were quite high, even for Africans. (This would be in contrast to other middle-income countries, rather than comparing, say, to postintegration United States.) However, the quality for Africans was very low. Africans tended to pass the high-school leaving exam at about half the rate that whites did, and many did not even make it to grade twelve to take the exam.

Next, there is a very important factor that is extremely difficult for western audiences to understand or, rather, extremely difficult to internalize deeply in terms of policy and political implications: In South Africa it is the *majority* that is nonwhite and poor. Thus, creating more equality of resourcing is not a simple matter of the rich making some small sacrifices and adaptations. To put it starkly, bringing the traditionally poorer African schools up to the traditional standards of resourcing of the white schools (swimming pools, tennis courts, etc.) was largely a fiscal impossibility, because the majority of the tax payers, not the minority as in the United States, are poor. It would have been impossible to level up, even under fairly lenient fiscal conditions, because the problem is not the willingness to tax, but the fact that the (national) tax base is composed mostly of poor citizens.

On top of everything, the last white government had essentially let loose the fiscal accounts and had increased government spending. The new democratic government therefore saw a need for macroeconomic belt-tightening, in which it engaged with considerable zeal—and without any known pressure from outside agencies. It was a home-grown austerity program.

Thus, under the circumstances, leveling had to be down, to a large degree, not up, as would be possible (if the political will existed) in the rich West, where the poor and nonwhite tend to be minorities. In the rich West, all or most progressive policy or political attitudes are deeply conditioned by the fact that leveling up is

fiscally feasible and would be largely a matter of political will, and it is very difficult for progressive westerners to give up this almost "genetic" predisposition to
think in terms of "adequacy" and to realize that, at least within the bounds of fiscal
responsibility, western-style leveling up was simply not doable in South Africa.

Finally, it has to be noted that South Africa is a fairly decentralized country,
where provinces ran the education systems, not the national government. Also, to a
degree unknown in the United States, each school has considerable financial and
governance autonomy.

So, what were some of the solutions devised by the new, democratic government? In the first place, the drive toward equity was undeniable, so pro-poor
spending policies were soon put in place, or at least the pro-rich spending policies
were stopped. This took place largely through four mechanisms. First, the national
government gave provincial governments block grants that were largely popula-
tion-based, with some favoring of poor areas. Whole provinces with strong African (poor) majorities suddenly received as much fiscal revenue per child as provinces with much larger proportions of white population, whereas in the past
resources were targeted by race, so areas with larger proportions of white population received more funding. This created a tremendous redistribution of resources
so that, within just five or six years, there had been an improvement of some 60
percent in some measures of interprovincial inequality. A shift of this magnitude is
probably unparalleled in any system that we are aware of. These reforms were the
first to be carried out, in 1995, almost immediately after the transition.

Second, teachers began to be allocated largely by enrollment, as opposed to
white schools being allocated more teachers. There was some residual favoring of
ex-white schools because the teacher-allocation formula favored the teaching of
certain specialized subjects with lower pupil-teacher ratios, and these subjects
were more commonly found in the ex-white schools. This caused fairly drastic increases in the ratio of publicly paid teachers to students in the ex-white schools,
usually from below twenty to one to above thirty-five to one. These policies were
phased in over the period 1996 to 1998.

Third, nonteaching resources were actively targeted toward the poor through
simple tables of allocation that required that, say, 65 percent of nonteaching,
noncapital resources reach the poorest 40 percent of the population. This was the
first attempt to proactively practice "positive" or pro-poor discrimination. It is important to note that the postapartheid discrimination, at least in the schooling system, was poverty based and not based on reversing the use of race as an allocation
mechanism. This was partly ideological, in the sense that the new government had
a commitment to nonracialism. But it also made technocratic sense: The richest,
ex-white schools were rapidly becoming integrated, but typically with the richer
Africans, and there was little sense in subsidizing rich Africans. Thus, the positive
discrimination was made race-blind and poverty-targeted. This policy was phased
in starting in 2000.

Fourth, and eventually, teacher allocations themselves started to shift toward a pro-poor allocation. This did not take place without considerable debate. Many analysts had pointed out that while allocating teachers with reference to enrollment seemed fair, not all teachers cost the same, and the most-trained and most-expensive teachers were still teaching in the privileged (although no longer white-reserved) schools. A certain percentage of the teaching pool was thus to be set aside to be allocated according to the same pro-poor resource targeting table as was used for the nonpersonnel resources. This reform was instituted in 2003.

There were two interesting reforms that were very controversial and are bound to seem very strange to a western audience. Recall that South Africa had an education system that was more than 95 percent public. There was, and still is, a serious desire to keep things that way. Public schools could be seen as key to nation-building and as centers of community life. However, the experience of post desegregation United States (especially in cities) and of Latin America was kept in mind. As resources were being stripped away from the better-off public schools, the fear was that the better off in society would "flee" to the private schools, creating a large market for private education. There was a fear that this would deprive the public education sector of powerful supporters, such as legislators, editorialists in the media, union leaders, and so forth, who would now all have their children in private schools. The belief is that personal commitment, in the sense of having one's own children in public schools, rather than ideological commitment, is the key to a healthy public school system. The fear was that middle- class flight would not only undermine budgetary support for public education but would deprive the public sector of its most discerning and demanding clients, and hence would deprive the public sector of accountability pressure based on real, personal experience as opposed to ideological commitment.

The solution struck was to permit parents in schools to self-assess fees within those schools, so as to support schools (e.g., hire extra teachers). Poor children were exempt on a sliding scale, and in any case children could not be kept from school if the parents did not pay the fees, but parents could indeed pressure each other to pay. Using this system, it was felt, public resources could be stripped from the rich schools and sent to the poorer schools (leveling down, a fiscal inevitability), but private resources could be brought to bear within the better-off public schools, keeping the well-off engaged with the public sector. It was fully realized that this would allow inequality within the public sector, but it was felt that it would still result in less overall (public and private) inequality and would also keep powerful stakeholders within the public sector, defending it and holding it accountable.

The other controversial policy was to subsidize private schools. This policy seems contradictory to the policy aimed at keeping education as public as possible. However, private schools, as noted, had actually been the most progressive during the period of apartheid and there was some sense among the new elites that this progressiveness needed to be recognized. Furthermore, many private schools did (and do) cater to the poor. Thus, the policies toward private school subsidization were fairly consciously aimed at two ends. First, they still created an advantage for the public schools, in that the subsidies were geared so as not to allow private schools (even including presumed private funding) to reach levels of per child spending common in public schools. Second, the subsidies were poverty-targeted, in that schools charging lower fees were given bigger subsidies. Schools charging the highest fees receive no subsidy—a policy that caused debate and acrimony with the private school sector.

What Happened?

What were the results as of about 2003? First, indexes of inequality were greatly improved. As noted, interprovincial inequality was reduced by some 60 percent. Our calculations, using concentration indexes, are that overall inequality (interprovincial and intraprovincial) was reduced from an index value of inequality in the allocation of public resources of 0.26 in 1991 to an index value of 0.027 by 2003.[3] It is interesting to consider how much inequality the allowance of private fees in public schools introduces: apparently not much. If one considers private and public resources together, the inequality index stands at 0.057 instead of 0.027. (Fees were close to zero in 1991 so the index value of 0.26 in public resource allocation is a fair indication of the inequality of total resource allocation in that year.) A level of 0.057 is undesirably high, but it is much, much lower than the 0.26 that existed before the end of apartheid.

In the meantime, the "trick" of using these fees to prevent the flight of the rich to private schools has worked. Schooling in South Africa, unlike, say, Latin America, is still nearly 95 percent public. While it is undeniably true that the ex-white, increasingly integrated but still rich public schools use far more resources than the poorer schools, because they can bring private resources to bear, it is also true that the issue of public education moves public officials, union leaders, and opinion-makers in a personal way that is totally different from what one finds in other middle-income countries and even in some U.S. cities, where the commitment to public education tends to be more ideological than personal, since few high-level officials have their own children in public schools. The well-off in South Africa still have both the duty and the privilege of participating in the public space that is a public school and in institutions that are governed by citizens. They tend not to simply hand off their children to professionals at a school that, because it is private, is not collectively governed and where therefore there are none of the democratic rituals and practices associated with running the small republic that a public school can be.

The system nonetheless has serious problems, and it is at some of these problems that the 2003 Review was aimed. The remainder of this review explains some of the more interesting and important of these issues. First, the fact that fees persist at the poorer schools militates against the pro-poor discrimination the public funding system aims at. By "twisting" the public funding system toward the poor it was thought the poor would not vote themselves fees at the schools they frequent, but for various reasons they persist. Sometimes this has to do perhaps with manipulation of the system by principals and teachers or by not-so-poor minorities of parents. The government recommended declaring the 40 percent of the poorest schools as "no-fee" schools, but subject to itself meeting its own commitment of making a minimum level of public resources available. In the previous funding system the government had committed itself to making 65 percent of the funding for nonpersonnel resources available to the poorest 40 percent of the schools but without actually guaranteeing an amount. The new policy recommends guaranteeing an amount to the poorest schools and declaring them no-fee schools.

Second, in the original formulation, the central (national) government had imposed the pro-poor spending on the provinces, but out of constitutional deference for provincial autonomy, so as not to create unfunded mandates, it had forced each province to spend 65 percent of its resources on *its own* 40 percent poorest schools. This raised the problem that the poorest schools in a rich province might seem fairly well off to a poorer province. The recommendation then was to make the poverty-targeting national in scope.

Third, in the original formulation each province was also allowed to determine which environmental variables to use in deciding each school's poverty—for example, proportion of the population in the district with access to electricity, literacy level of the parental generation in the school's catchment area, and so forth. It was felt that in poorer provinces factors such as whether schools had libraries would not allow for distinctions between poverty levels because no schools had them. In other areas, whether schools had electricity also would not work because all schools had them. But if poverty is now a national criterion, the same factors are to be used uniformly, and the determination is to be made in collaboration with the country's central statistical agency, not by each provincial department of education. These recommendations are made in the Review.

Fourth, as in the United States, there has been considerable debate about the fact that, despite increased funding, school performance does not always improve. Despite massive efforts to redistribute resources toward the poor, results were not following. Thus, the Review calls for improved school monitoring, measurement, and accountability. This is probably one of the more difficult recommendations, in that implementing it requires much more complex quality assurance systems than the financial recommendations suggested previously. It was also felt that part of the problem was that while funding was being reallocated, the professional quality of teachers in poor schools was not what it should be. The Review thus also recommends improving support to teachers, and making the necessary allocations, while expecting more from them in terms of accountability and monitoring of performance.

Few countries in the world have made as dedicated and original an attempt to address funding equity as South Africa, and few have been as willing to deeply review their own performance quickly and forthrightly. The Review was carried out only five years after the new policies were put in place. While results in terms of equity have improved vastly, they could improve more. While equity of results has also started to improve, the performance of poor schools, particularly in the early grades and in the basic skills, still requires vast improvement.

Notes

1. It has to be understood that this is a report *from* the Department of Education *to* the Minister of Education. In the context of South Africa's style of government, this is a report from the bureaucracy to the political head of the sector; the Minister may or may not accept the recommendations. Thus, even though it is a document produced by the bureaucracy, it does not necessarily become government policy until the recommendations are accepted by the Cabinet.

2. The author, funded by United States Agency for International Development (USAID), worked as advisor to the government of South Africa on many of the reforms discussed herein.

3. These index values refer to Gini coefficients (or more rigorously concentration indexes) where a theoretical limit of 1 exists in a totally unequal society where one person owns all of the resources and the rest of society owns none, to 0 indicating total equality, to less than zero where the poor receive more of a public resource than the rich. At the theoretical negative extreme of −1, the poorest person in the society receives all of a resource. In the latter case the resource in question has to be a public resource or transfer, not private income, of course, or else that person would not be the poorest, by definition.

ACKNOWLEDGMENT

I would like to thank Martin Gustafsson for helping prioritize the main results of the Review.

TIME EXPOSURE

Lewis Wickes Hine (1874–1940) was the preeminent photographer of the child labor movement in the United States. He first began to work as a photographer while teaching at the Ethical Culture School in New York. His famous series of photographs of Ellis Island, including the "Madonna of Ellis Island," were taken as part of a field trip with his students. In 1906 he began to work for the National Child Labor Committee (NCLC) and in 1908 was hired by them full time. For approximately ten years Hine roamed the United States for the NCLC researching articles and documenting through his photography the conditions of child labor and poverty in the United States. His photographs of children working in mines, factories, canneries, textile mills, street trades, and assorted agricultural industries

Jack Ryan, 6 years old, and Jesse Ryan, 10 years old. Onem Smith, 12 years old and lives at 1506 S. Robinson St. Onem said: "I never have been in school in my life but I got a pretty good education—sellin papers." Been selling here 6 months. Photograph by Lewis W. Hine, of truants in Oklahoma City, Oklahoma, taken March 14, 1917.

played a critical role in changing public attitudes about child labor and lead to the implementation of major child labor laws at the time of the First World War. The above photograph of newspaper boys truant from school in Oklahoma City, Oklahoma, taken in March 1917, is typical of his photographs.

Additional materials can be found at the Time Exposures site:

Time Exposures: Visual Explorations in the History of American Education
http://www.education.miami.edu/ep/Time%20Exposures/index.html

Eugene F. Provenzo, Jr.
University of Miami

BOOKS AVAILABLE LIST

For a complete list of all titles available, go to
http://www3.uakron.edu/aesa/publications/edstudies.html

BOOKS RECEIVED WINTER 2005/2006

Adams, Natalie G., Christine Mary Shea, Delores D. Liston, and Bryan Deever. *Learning to Teach: A Critical Approach to Field Experiences,* 2nd ed. Mahwah, N.J.: Lawrence Erlbaum Associates, Inc., 2006. 162 pp. $26.00 (paper).

Apple, Michael W., and Kristen L. Buras, eds. *The Subaltern Speak: Curriculum, Power, and Educational Struggles.* New York: Routledge Taylor & Francis Group, 2006. 294 pp. $24.95 (paper).

Brantlinger, Ellen A., ed. *Who Benefits From Special Education?* Mahwah, N.J.: Lawrence Erlbaum Associates, Inc., 2006. 261 pp. $27.50 (paper).

Gutstein, Eric. *Reading and Writing the World with Mathematics.* New York: Routledge Taylor & Francis Group, 2006. 257 pp. $21.90 (paper).

Hughes, Sherick A., ed. *What We Still Don't Know About Teaching Race: How To Talk About It In The Classroom.* Lewiston, N.Y.: The Edwin Mellen Press, 2005. 444 pp. $129.95 (cloth).

Nash, Margaret A. *Women's Education in the United States 1780–1840.* New York: Palgrave Macmillan, 2006. 203 pp. $28.95 (paper).

Pace, Judith L., and Annette Hemmings, eds. *Classroom Authority: Theory, Research, and Practice.* Mahwah, N.J.: Lawrence Erlbaum Associates, Inc., 2006. 193 pp. $24.50 (paper).

Pumpian, Ian, Douglas Fisher, and Susan Wachowiak. *Challenging the Classroom Standard Through Museum-Based Education.* Mahwah, N.J.: Lawrence Erlbaum Associates, Inc., 2006. 160 pp. $21.50 (paper).

Shapiro, H. Svi. *Losing Heart: The Moral and Spiritual Miseducation of America's Children.* Mahwah, N.J.: Lawrence Erlbaum Associates, Inc., 2006. 224 pp. $22.50 (paper).

Sidhu, Ravinder K. *Universitites and Globalization: To Market, To Market.* Mahwah, N.J.: Lawrence Erlbaum Associates, Inc., 2006. 360 pp. $45.00 (paper).

Smith, Debbie, and Kathryn F. Whitmore. *Literacy and Advocacy in Adolescent Family, Gang, School, and Juvenile Court Communities.* Mahwah, N.J.: Lawrence Erlbaum Associates, Inc., 2006. 203 pp. $24.50 (paper).

For Product Safety Concerns and Information please contact our EU
representative GPSR@taylorandfrancis.com Taylor & Francis Verlag GmbH,
Kaufingerstraße 24, 80331 München, Germany

Batch number: 08153776

Printed by Printforce, the Netherlands